THE ULTIMATE JOKE BOOK

100s *of Great Clean Jokes*

by Dan Harmon

HUMBLECREEK
INSPIRATION FOR LIFE

ISBN 1-58660-077-X

Published by Humble Creek, P.O. Box 719, Uhrichsville, Ohio 44683

 Member of the
Evangelical Christian
Publishers Association

Printed in the United States of America.

CONTENTS

INTRODUCTION

You deserve a good laugh today—something to melt away stress, burn off some calories, and leave you feeling tingly all over. God gave you laughter as a gift—take advantage of it!

In this book, you'll find plenty to make you chuckle, snicker, cackle—or maybe even snort. Jokes of all sorts, guaranteed to crack a smile on the face of even the most humor-challenged person, will keep you in stitches (but preferably not the medical kind!).

Get ready, sit back, and relax. . .with *The Ultimate Joke Book*, a sure-fire way to tickle your funny bone. With hundreds of jokes, you're in for hours of enjoyment!

AGE

Two children were caught in mischief by their grandmother. Happily, she chose not to punish them. "I remember being young once, too," she mused.

"Gee, Grandma," said one of the children, wide-eyed. "You sure have an incredible memory!"

The grandparents listened respectfully as little Sherman described what he'd learned in history class. "We saw a video of the first man landing on the moon! His name was Neil Armstrong."

Grandpa turned to Grandma. "*History?* I thought that was current events."

"Grandma, what did you get for your birthday when you were a little girl?"

"Oh, we were very poor. We didn't get many birthday gifts. We were content just to get a year older."

"What causes old age, Grandpa?"
"Living."

Did you hear about the latest government study on aging? It cost $240 million and provided compelling evidence that the average American is growing older.

A ninety-five-year-old gentleman entered a life insurance office and told the agent he wanted to take out a $300,000 whole-life policy.

"But you're simply too old," the agent said after a moment's consideration. "No insurance company would start a new policy on a ninety-five-year-old client."

"Sonny boy," the applicant steamed, "are you aware of the mortality demographics within the United States of America?"

"Why, yes, Sir. I believe I know the statistics pretty well."

"What percentage of the population is known to die between the ages of 90 and 120?"

"Er, something less than 5 percent. . ."

"Then what, exactly, is your problem with my age bracket?"

The agent wrote the policy.

"Dad, what's middle age?"

"That's when you lose all your growth at the top and do all your growing in the middle."

An elderly man took his faithful but weather-beaten Packard to a tune-up shop for an oil change. The two mechanics exchanged glances as the car puttered to a stop at the garage door.

"Man," said one with a low whistle, "I'll bet that thing's still insured against Indian attack."

"I think the older my grandpa gets," a girl remarked to a friend, "the farther he had to walk to school when he was my age."

A widow was describing to a friend the gentleman she'd recently been dating.

"Does he wear his hair parted or unparted?" her friend asked.

"Actually. . .departed."

A nonagenarian was interviewed by a local newspaper reporter. "Do you have a lot of great-grandchildren?" the reporter asked.

"To tell the truth," confessed the matriarch, "I expect they're all pretty ordinary."

AIRPLANES

The transatlantic flight to England was halfway across when the pilot came on the intercom with a casual message to the passengers. "You may have noticed a slight change in the sound of the engines. That's because we've had to shut down Engine Two temporarily. There's no cause for concern; we have three more engines in fine condition. But there'll be a slight delay. Our expected time of arrival has been changed from 2:14 P.M. to 2:45 P.M. Sorry for any inconvenience that may cause."

An hour later the pilot was back on the intercom, chuckling softly. "Folks, this is the first time I've ever experienced this, and I never thought it would happen, but we seem to have lost power in Engine Four. No problem in terms of safety, but we'll have a further delay. We now expect to arrive at Heathrow International at 3:30 P.M."

And a little while later he was back at the mike, still trying to sound reassuring but with an edge in his voice. "You won't believe this, but Engine One seems to be on the blink, and we've decided it's wise to shut it down. This is a weird situation, but not really alarming. We can easily finish the flight with one engine, although we'll be flying substantially slower. We now anticipate arriving around 4:25."

One passenger turned to another and mumbled, "If that last engine goes out, it'll be next Tuesday till we get to England."

The first-time flier was not assured when the flight attendant cheerily pointed out that the passenger seat could be removed and used as a flotation device. "I'd much rather be sitting on a parachute," he remarked to the person next to him.

"I'd like an aisle seat on the 3:30 flight to Dayton, please," a richly dressed woman told her travel agent.

The agent studied the computer database and frowned. "Hmm. I can get you aboard that flight, but only in a window seat."

"No, no. I never sit by the window. I won't have my hair blown all out of place."

The first-time flier was very nervous as he buckled his seatbelt before takeoff. He turned to the woman in the next seat and asked, "About how often do jetliners like this crash?"

She thought a moment and replied, "About once, usually."

After watching a news account of an airline crash, a teenager was asking his mother about the vital "black box" that's so important to accident investigators.

"It contains a complete record of the plane's diagnostics right up to the instant of the crash," she explained.

"Why isn't it destroyed on impact?"

"Because it's encased in a very special alloy material, I'm sure."

"Then why can't they make the whole airplane out of that material?"

A man edged his way down the aisle to what he thought was his row aboard a jetliner awaiting takeoff. He looked at his ticket, then at the gentleman sitting by the window, then back at his ticket, then back at the gentleman.

"I have 17-F," he stated, getting the other's attention. "I believe you're in my seat."

"No, I'm in 17-D. Says so right here." He took out his own ticket and showed it to the man in the aisle.

"Yes, but 17-D is the aisle seat. You see, the seating runs from side to side, A-B-C and then D-E-F. A and F are the window seats, and C and D are the aisle seats."

"Nonsense. I asked them for a window seat, so this must be it. Seat 17-D, Flight 501 to St. Louis."

"Oh. Then you're definitely out of place. All the seats going to St. Louis are in the middle row."

For $10, visitors to the country fair could ride in a barnstormer's biplane. An aging farm couple who'd never traveled outside the county thought they might like to take the opportunity to fly, just for posterity. But they were more than a little afraid.

"Tell you what," the barnstormer offered, perceiving their nervousness. "You can ride together, and I'll charge you only $5. Just promise me you won't scream or try to tell me how to fly my plane."

They accepted his offer and proceeded with the thrill of their lives. Through a wild series of loops and rolls, the pilot never heard a sound from his backseat companions.

"Wow, Pop, you were just great!" shouted the pilot over his shoulder as he landed the plane. "I thought for sure you'd both holler when we made that nosedive."

"That wasn't so bad," yelled the farmer. "But I almost did break my promise a few minutes before that when my wife fell out of the airplane."

A teenager approached an airline ticket desk at the Indianapolis airport to inquire about an afternoon flight to Seattle. Without explaining the different time zones to him—Seattle is three hours behind—the agent punched a few keys on the computer and announced, "You can catch a flight at 5:02 P.M. nonstop to Seattle. It arrives at 5:24."

The youth rubbed his chin. "The plane leaves here at 5:02 and gets to Seattle at 5:24?"

"Yes."

"Today?"

"That's correct. Would you like to purchase a ticket?"

"No, I think I'll walk over there and watch that plane take off one time."

Navy jet pilot: "This is it! We're flying faster than the speed of sound!"
Copilot: "What?"

A rookie flight attendant was so nervous he was dropping trays, spilling drinks on passengers, and stumbling into his colleagues in the aisles.

"Calm down," said another attendant, drawing him aside in the galley. "You're behaving as if you've never flown before."

"I've flown lots of times," he responded. "But this afternoon before we took off, I got to examine all the restricted areas of the plane for the first time in my life. Just looking around gave me a terrible panic attack."

"Why? It's just another airliner."

"Don't you realize," he said, "that virtually every little part of this thing was supplied by the lowest bidder?"

A nervous passenger decided to spring for one of those on-the-spot, low-investment-high-benefits insurance policies at the airport before her plane departed. Then she had time for a quick lunch, so she stopped at a Chinese dinery along the terminal walk. Her eyes widened when she read the fortune cookie: "Today's investment will pay big dividends!"

A flight attendant was surprised to hear a loud burst of laughter in the cockpit. A few seconds later, there was another outburst. Then a third.

The attendant opened the door to see what was going on. "What's the joke?"

"Oh, it's nothing, really," said the pilot. "I just get tickled when I imagine what the warden's gonna say when he discovers I've escaped from prison."

"Would you please bring me some cotton balls?" an airline pilot asked a flight attendant as the plane began its landing approach.

"The change in air pressure hurts your ears, huh?" guessed the attendant with an understanding smile.

"No. But the yelling and shrieking will after I inform the passengers our landing gear won't go down and we have to do a belly slide."

ANiMALS

A vacationing family rented a van at a drive-through wild animal reserve. One of the children was disgusted by the barred windows, welded in place for passengers' protection. "Isn't there a law against putting families in cages?" she asked.

"Dad, don't we get leather from cows?"
   "That's right, Son."
   "Doesn't leather shrink when it gets wet?"
   "Usually."
   "Then what happens to cows when they stand outside in the rain?"

Two elephants were discussing life in general on Planet Earth.
   "You know," said one, "we're considered by human scientists to possess the best memories of any animals on the face of the globe."
   "Well, darn," said the other. "Why can't I remember where I left my bag of peanuts?"

Two snakes were camouflaged in the jungle, feeding on passing insects. One remarked to the other, "Time's sure fun when we're having flies."

ART

A critic scowled up and down the aisles of a modern art exhibit. He stopped before one particularly abstract work.

"What in the world is that supposed to be?" he wondered aloud.

"That," said the artist, who happened to be standing nearby, "is 'supposed to be' the Great Wall of China at sundown."

"Then why isn't it?" snapped the critic.

There's an easy way to understand modern art. If it's hanging on a wall, it's a picture. If you can walk around it, it's probably a sculpture.

André Gide once defined art as a collaboration between an artist and God—"and the less the artist does, the better."

ATTITUDES

Grandpa had been in a fussy mood, snapping at the grandchildren all day. That night Grandma gave him a stern lecture about his intolerance.

"Oh, I enjoy children well enough," he defended. "I used to go to school with some of 'em."

Mrs. Avondale was walking an interior designer through the mansion, discussing renovations. The professional had many fine suggestions, and Mrs. Avondale accepted them all with the sweep of a hand.

"I only demand one thing," she said, turning to the designer. "When my best friend Marguerite comes in here after we're finished, I want her to drop dead from envy."

Four cowboys were gambling for high stakes in an Old West saloon. One spread out four kings and proclaimed haughtily, "Looks like I win."

"Nope," growled another. "You don't win."

"What've you got?" demanded the first cowboy, astonished.

"Pair o' jacks and a Colt .45."

The first gambler pounded the table angrily. "It just ain't right. You been havin' all the luck."

AUTOMOBILES

A woman waited at a garage as mechanics scoured her car engine, trying in vain to pinpoint the problem. At length, a parrot in a corner cage sang out, "It's the thermostat."

"We've already checked the thermostat," grumbled one of the mechanics.

"It's the fan belt," the parrot ventured.

"No problem with the fan belt," said the other mechanic.

"It's the heat pump," said the parrot.

"It's not the heat pump!" shouted the first mechanic, exasperated.

The woman was astounded by this exchange. "I've never heard of a bird so intelligent," she said.

"He's completely worthless," countered the second mechanic. "He'll talk your ear off, but he doesn't know the first thing about car engines."

Two street people were being entertained watching a teenager try to park a car across the street. The space was ample, but the driver just couldn't maneuver the car into it. Traffic was jammed. Angry drivers honked, further flabbergasting the poor youth. It took a full five minutes before the car was in place.

"That," said one of the idlers, "is what you call paralyzed parking."

A rich suburbanite had car trouble while on a mountain holiday. He puttered into the yard of a rickety roadside filling station and called to the greasy, bearded attendant, "Have you had any experience with BMWs?"

"Buddy, if I could work on cars like that, I don't reckon I'd be here."

"The earth is round," the teacher said, "which means the surface of the earth is gradually curved."

"That explains it!" shouted Marcia.

"Explains what?"

"That explains why Mom's car pulls to the right."

BASEBALL

A losing pitcher approached his catcher outside the locker room. "Let me borrow a quarter," he said. "I promised one of my fans I'd phone after the game."

The catcher searched his pockets. "I only have a dollar bill. Here, take it. Now you can phone all your fans."

A fan was starstruck with the opportunity to actually speak to his professional baseball idol. "Have you played baseball from the very beginning?" the fan gushed.

"Not while I was a baby," the player intoned.

One baseball fan said to another at the beginning of the season, "I don't wanna sound pessimistic, but our guys are gonna get annihilated by the Orioles."

"No way," said the other. "They'll whip the Orioles and every other team in the league."

"I wish. This year, though, I really don't think they could whip cream."

BIRDS

Several buzzards had been circling all day, looking for a dead animal carcass to eat. As night approached, one wearily suggested to the others, "Let's just kill some small animal and eat it. If we don't, we'll all die of starvation."

"Buzzards can't do that," croaked a second.

"Says who?"

"I read it in the nature encyclopedia."

A duck waddled into a country grocery store and asked the clerk, "Do you sell duck food?"

"Of course not," replied the clerk. "We sell groceries to humans, not ducks."

The next day, the duck returned and asked again, "Do you sell duck food?"

Annoyed, the clerk snapped, "No! No duck food."

When the duck returned the next day and posed the same question, the clerk threatened, "I've told you this is a grocery store for people, not birds. If you ever come back in here and ask me that stupid question again, I'm going to nail one of your webbed feet to the floor and laugh while you walk around in circles."

The next day the duck was back. "Do you sell nails?"

The clerk, miffed, replied, "Of course not. This is a grocery store, not a hardware store."

Upon which the duck asked, "Do you sell duck food?"

Two women sat on a park bench. One was immersed in the newspaper, the other admiring the beauty of the falling orange leaves, the cool September breeze, the squirrels chattering, and a million birds singing. "Oh, this is so wonderful," she couldn't help remarking. "Don't you just love the music of the birds?"

The other turned to her with a questioning frown. "Couldn't hear what you said. Can't hear anything at all with these obnoxious birds and squirrels making such a racket."

CARPENTERS

Dad was pounding furiously with a hammer on a back porch wood project. Dogs barked. Neighbors phoned to complain. Items hanging on the wall were rocked off their mounts.

His two children watched as the family's portable weather station crashed to the floor. One child turned to the other and asked, "Is this what weather broadcasters mean when they say the barometer is falling?"

A residential building contractor went to a lumberyard and told the stock clerk he needed a truckload of two-by-fours.

"How long?" asked the clerk.

"I'll need 'em about forty or fifty years, I guess."

A policeman watched suspiciously as a man stepped out of a van, holding his hands about two feet apart. The man hurried down the street; the policeman followed. At the entrance to a building supply store, the suspect—hands still apart—waited until a customer came through the door. He darted through the open door behind the other person, seemingly afraid to touch the door with either hand.

The officer quietly entered the store behind him, just in time to hear the stranger tell a clerk, "I need half a dozen three-by-fours cut exactly this long."

At a building site, a load of suspended lumber broke from a hoist and fell to the ground, burying a carpenter. Before his shocked coworkers could get to him, he rose from the rubble, dusted his overalls, and hollered at the crane operator, "You idiot! You made me bite my lip!"

A foreman making the rounds of a building site suddenly noticed one of his laziest workers was absent—again. "Hey, where's Sparkman?" he shouted.

"You must've missed his funeral," said a coworker. "He's been dead and buried more than a month."

CELEBRITIES & DIGNITARIES

Two rival candidates for a local government seat happened to meet at a taxi stand. Smith was a wealthy veteran of city hall politics, Brown a middle-income political novice.

"I hate to tell you this, Son," said Smith, condescending to offer a bit of frank advice, "but you need money if you ever want to run a successful campaign in this city. *Lots* of money. See this?" He took a wad of bills from a coat pocket. "I always carry plenty of cash and spread it around liberally. For example, when my cabby drops me off, I'll give him a wink, a smile, and a $5 bill, and let him know I'm counting on his vote."

Young Brown got to thinking about the tactic and came up with a shoestring-budget variation. When his own cab driver dropped him off, he quickly stepped out the door without leaving any tip at all. "Be sure to vote for Smith in the city council race next Tuesday," he called over his shoulder.

The successful novelist, being interviewed on a TV talk show, lamented of burnout and self-doubt. "After twelve books and $7–8 million dollars in royalties, I finally realize I haven't the slightest talent for writing. Every one of my plots is just a rehash of things I've read by other writers."

"Are you telling us," hazarded the host, "that you're retiring?"

"Oh, of course not! Imagine what that would do to my reputation!"

Throngs of admirers collected around the handsome actor at a shopping mall.

"Is that a real mustache?" one child asked.

"No, not this one. I keep my real one at home on the dresser."

One candidate at a political rally held the podium a full forty minutes with what had to be the most meaningless, boring speech in the county's history. Finally, he concluded and asked if anyone in the audience had a question.

"I do," piped up a voice. "Who's your opponent?"

The actor was talented, but unknown. A few minor roles in commercials and Grade B films were encouraging to his ego. But the fact was, he couldn't make his monthly rent payment.

"Don't you realize," he explained to his pragmatic landlord, "that within a year or two, my fans will be flocking to this address, just to view the apartment where such a great talent once lived?"

"I expect my rent in two days," said the landlord. "If I don't get paid, on the third day, your fans may proceed to come around and view the apartment where you once lived."

An actor once rose to accept an award. "Don't worry," he began. "I won't speak very long. This tuxedo is due back in half an hour."

A candidate and his wife fell into the hotel bed at the end of a long day on the campaign trail.

"I'm exhausted," groaned the wife.

"I think I have more right to be exhausted than you do," complained the candidate. "I delivered six speeches in six no-count little towns today."

"And I had to listen to the same message six times."

The politician concluded a boisterous but shallow speech filled with impossible promises sure to appeal to the particular audience. Mingling with the crowd, he happened on a wise, respected old city father. Hoping for a compliment within hearing of some of the audience, he asked the old man what he thought of the speech.

"Well," the gentleman said thoughtfully, "I think for those who want to hear about those kinds of things, those were exactly the kinds of statements they wanted to hear."

CHILDREN

Father: "You never know what you can do until you try."
Son: "I guess you never know what you *can't* do until you try, either."

Mandy came crying to her dad. Between sobs, she explained that she'd traded her pet kitten Jingles to the children at the refreshment stand down the street for a cold drink.

"I see," he said, knowingly. "And now you miss little Jingles, don't you?"

"No," she said, "but I'm still thirsty, and I don't have anything else to trade?"

A jolly department store Santa Claus took a small girl on his knee and asked, "Now tell me the first thing you plan to do Christmas morning."

She thought, scratched her head, and replied, "Wake up."

After being punished for losing his temper, a little boy ventured to say to his mother, "Please explain to me the difference between my foul temper and your worn nerves."

Two mothers were comparing child-rearing notes. "I just can't seem to get my children's attention," said one. "They stay mesmerized in front of the TV set. I say things to them and call for them, and they're oblivious to every word."

"Try sitting in an easy chair and looking like you're relaxed," said the other. "That gets my children's attention without fail."

Little Kristin, five, was showing a neighborhood friend around her house. Her friend had never seen bathroom scales before and was mystified by the dial.

"What is this?" the friend asked.

"I'm not really sure. But I know what it's used for. It's a machine that puts grown-up people in a terrible mood."

Michelle: "My parents have dreadful memories."
Chris: "Can't remember everything, huh?"
Michelle: "Oh, no. That's the problem. They *do* remember everything."

The tradition in the farm family was that when one of the boys misbehaved, he got a switching. And to drive the point home, he was required to go outside and cut his own switch.

Thus, bad little Ernie was sent out the door to select his means of punishment. Gone for several minutes, he finally returned with no switch—but with a handful of rocks.

"I couldn't find a good switch for you, Pa," he said. "Why don't you just stone me?"

A schoolteacher phoned the home of one of her students. The father answered.

"I just wanted to ask if there's anything I can do," the teacher said compassionately.

"Er, I don't think so. I believe we have everything under control."

"Well, Jessi told me yesterday she would need to miss classes today because her mother's dying."

There was a long silence. "So, I take it Jessi wasn't at school today?" the father asked suspiciously.

"Oh, no. I naturally told her she could be excused."

The parents immediately confronted their daughter. "You told your teacher I was dying!" the mother shouted. "That was a terrible lie. You know I'm perfectly well. Why, I was working all day, as usual, except for a quick trip to the beauty shop."

"Yep," Jessi said sweetly. "You were going to have your hair dyed. That's basically what I told the teacher."

A father was scolding his children because they spent most of their summer days watching television. "Don't you know laziness is a trap? You'll never amount to anything if you fall into lazy habits. It's hard work that pays off."

The oldest child replied, "I know it'll pay off when we grow up. But for now, being lazy seems to pay off a lot better."

A little boy took the chair at the barber shop.

"How would you like your hair cut today, Son?" asked the barber.

"Oh, do it like you do Daddy's, with the big hole at the back."

Micki's parents received a disturbing note from her second-grade teacher:

"Micki is an excellent student," the teacher began, "but when we have art and coloring projects, she draws everything in dark blue. Sky, grass, flowers, people, houses, kittens, cars, buildings, sun, moon, trees—it's all dark blue. This is unusual for a second-grader. Can you think of any explanation? If she's having some sort of emotional problem, we need to get to the bottom of it."

That night, the parents sat down with Micki and asked her why all her pictures were rendered in dark blue. Why was that such a special color to her? they asked.

"Well," she began, "I wasn't going to tell you. But see, about two weeks ago I lost my box of crayons. The only one left is the dark blue one I found in the front compartment of my book bag. . . ."

"I've never seen a hand so filthy," Mother said to Sammy when he came in from playing.

"Then take a look at this one," said Sammy, holding up his other hand.

Six-year-old Alison was riding in the car with her mother. Mom bumped the signal light lever and prepared to make a turn. Alison was annoyed by the clicking cadence the signal device emitted from the dashboard.

"Mom, why in the world do you turn that thing on?"

"To let other drivers know I'm going to turn, Dear."

"But Mom, nobody can hear it but you and me."

An eighth-grader was visibly frustrated as he struggled with his homework. Finally, he slammed the textbook shut, threw down his pencil, and announced to his parents, "I've decided I'm a conscientious objector."

"Why did you decide that?" his father asked.

"Because wars create too much history."

Thad: "Mom, I sure wish I had a new skateboard like Jerry's."

Mother: "You shouldn't spend your life wanting things other people have."

Thad: "But what other kinds of things are there to want?"

Carolyn: "Mom, will you give me enough money to buy three cartons of milk?"

Mother, suspiciously: "Why do you want to buy three cartons of milk? We have milk in the refrigerator."

Carolyn: "Well, I don't really want to buy three cartons of milk."

Mother: "Then why did you ask for that much money?"

Carolyn: "Because with that much money, I could buy the new doll they have at the toy store."

"But why can't I talk inside the library?" Mandy asked her mother.

"Because you have to be quiet. Noise is a distraction. The people around you can't read."

"Can't read? Then why are they at the library?"

The mother was furious. "Ricky," she called to her son, "last night when I turned out the kitchen light and went to bed, there were four Twinkie packages in the cookie jar. This morning there are only two. What do you know about this?"

"Well, it was kinda dark," Ricky confessed. "I only saw two packages."

"Oww!" screamed six-year-old Mindy.

"What is it?" her mother called from the kitchen.

"The baby pulled my hair."

Mother came in to comfort Mindy. "Don't be angry at the baby," she said. "He doesn't understand that it hurts when he pulls your hair."

She'd no sooner returned to the kitchen when there came another shriek, this time from the toddler. Returning to the playroom, she was confronted by Mindy, who explained, "Now he understands."

"How far away is the sun?" a child asked her father.

"I'm not sure, Honey."

"Well, how far away is the moon?"

"I don't know that, either."

"Do you know when the next solar eclipse will be?"

"Nope. Sorry."

"That's okay. Hope you don't mind me asking so many questions."

"Not at all. Asking questions is the only way to learn anything."

A small child worked up the courage to confront the neighborhood bully. "Bullies are really wimps," he told himself as he rounded a fence corner. "Show me a bully, and I'll show you a real wimp."

To his horror, there stood the bully—who'd overheard his self-psyching reverie.

"Show you a bully, huh?" the mean boy asked, sneering. "Well, right here's a bully for you."

The little foe screwed up his face and barked fiercely, "Yeah, and right here's a wimp for you!"

Grandaunt Sarah, in town for a visit, was having the most wonderful time talking with five-year-old Anne. "And have you been minding your table manners?" she asked.

"Oh, yes, Ma'am. Mommy has taught me all the rules, and I follow them whenever I can."

"What are some of the rules you've learned, my dear?"

"Well, like, don't throw food in other people's iced tea glasses."

A mother was trying to impress upon her children the need for safety while playing. "You remember our neighbor Barry," she said somberly. "He was riding his roller skates and wasn't paying attention where he was going. He hit a tree and ended up in the hospital, and now his right leg's paralyzed. He'll never skate again."

Little Jeannie was suddenly quite interested. "So what became of his skates?"

Two children were shouting at each other and were at the point of blows when Mom entered the playroom. "You two are always arguing," she scolded. "You need to learn to agree on things."

"We do agree," said one.

"Yeah," snarled the other. "We both agree we want the box of crayons *right now*."

A child was thoroughly bored after being stuck inside the house all day because of rain. "Mom," she whined, "why does God send the rain, anyway?"

"To nourish the earth," her mother said. "That's how the crops and the flowers and the trees grow."

"But why does He make it rain in the parking lot where I like to go skating?"

A mother came home from shopping and found her newly baked pie dug out crudely from the center. The crime tool—a gooey spoon—lay in the sink. Crumbs were all over the kitchen counter and floor.

She called her son into the kitchen. "Peter, she said sternly, you promised me you wouldn't touch that pie before dinner."

Peter hung his head.

"And I promised you I'd spank you if you did," she continued.

Peter brightened. "Now that I've broken my promise," he offered, "I think it'll be all right for you to break yours, too!"

CHURCH HUMOR

"Lord," came the prayer, "so far today, so good. I haven't sworn, stolen anything, boasted, gotten angry at anyone, or even had any evil thoughts.

"But now comes the test, and I implore Your help. I have to get up and go to work. . . ."

"Adam and Eve must have been extremely bored," a child told her parents, shaking her head.

"What makes you think that?" asked her father. "They lived in the Garden of Eden, which was a living paradise on earth."

"Yeah, but, like, they didn't have anybody to gossip about."

"King David used to be a hero of mine, but not anymore," little Brodie told his mother after church one Sunday.

"Why not, Son?"

"I learned today that he killed the Jolly Green Giant."

"Does anyone know the meaning of the word 'epistle'?" the Sunday school teacher asked.

"I believe those were the wives of the apostles," guessed one student.

Sharing the week's news while waiting for Sunday school to begin, a woman related to the gathering class members how old Arthur, a dear neighbor, had met his death. "He was trying to store something in the attic, apparently. They think he slipped on the top step, fell all the way down, hit his head on the floor, and died almost instantly of a concussion."

"Broke his specs, too," chipped in her husband.

Two children were among worshipers filing into the sanctuary the first Sunday morning in January. One frowned and pointed to the Christmas tree, which still stood in honor of the Advent season. "Why is the Christmas tree still up?"

"Because it isn't December 25th yet," the other child answered.

A family who'd just moved into town spent Sunday mornings for the first few months visiting different churches. Returning home after one service, the eight year old remarked, "We definitely don't wanna join that church."

"Why not?" asked Dad.

"This is the third time we've been there, and it's rained every time."

A child was watching his mother sift through and delete a long list of junk E-mail on the computer screen.

"This reminds me of the Lord's Prayer," the child said.

"What do you mean?"

"You know. That part about 'deliver us from E-mail.'"

Torrential rains were swiftly flooding the town's streets. A preacher sat on his porch watching the deluge. As the rising water approached his front steps, a rescue squad boat motored by. "Come aboard, Preacher!" shouted one of the officials. "We'll carry you to safety."

"I'm safe enough," the preacher replied. "I'm trusting the Lord to protect me and my home."

Half an hour later the water was up to the porch floor. Another boat glided past. "Jump aboard, Preacher! It's going to get worse!"

"I'm not afraid, Friends. The Lord will deliver me from drowning."

Late in the day, the flood had almost engulfed the town's buildings. The preacher was on the roof, clinging to the chimney, when a helicopter hovered overhead. A rope was cranked down to the pitiful victim—and astonishingly, the preacher waved the crew away. "The Lord Himself will save me," he declared.

And as darkness descended, the preacher was swept to his death.

The next thing he knew, he was at heaven's gate, waiting at the desk of St. Peter. The venerable saint looked up from his writing. "You!" he exclaimed. "What are you doing here already?" "Well," the preacher stammered, "I was down there in the flood, waiting for the Lord to rescue me, and finally the water just got too high and. . ."

"Saints, Man! We sent you two boats and a helicopter!"

Casey approached her Sunday school teacher after class with a question: "If the people of Israel were Israelites, and the people of Canaan were Canaanites, are Parasites what we call the people living in Paris?"

Who were the famous triplets of the New Testament?
First, Second, and Third John.

"Pastor, do you believe in ghosts?"

"No—not in the popular sense, at any rate. Why do you ask?"

"We're considering buying the old Carter mansion on South Main Street. It's a beautiful Victorian, and we'd love to restore it. But everyone says it's haunted by the ghost of old Mr. Carter."

"Well, my opinion is that if his soul's in hell, he can't return. If he's in heaven, he doesn't want to."

A country church held a covered dish supper on opening night of its revival series. The guest preacher was invited to lead the food line, but he declined. "I can't eat a big meal before I preach," he explained to the congregation. "It detracts from my ability to deliver a good sermon."

Two hours later, several women were cleaning up the church kitchen. "I declare," mumbled one, "I believe that preacher might as well have ate his fill at suppertime."

An older gentleman had a parcel weighed for shipment at the post office.

"Are any of the contents breakable?" asked the clerk.

"Depends on who you are, I suppose."

"What do you mean?"

"There's an antique Bible in that package. To me, the Ten Commandments are unbreakable. I can't speak for you, though."

Sunday school teacher: "What became of Tyre?"
Pupil: "The Lord punctured it."

"Can anyone name the Roman emperor who was most notorious for persecuting early Christians?" the Sunday school teacher asked.

"Nero," promptly responded one youth.

"That's right. What were some of the things he did?"

"He tortured the prisoners in Rome."

"And do you know how he tortured them?"

"He played the fiddle at 'em."

Little Rodney seemed troubled at Sunday dinner. "What is it, Son?" his dad asked.

"I really didn't like that violent hymn we sang in church," Rodney said.

"Violent? What hymn was violent?"

"You know. The one that goes, 'There is a bomb in Gilead.' "

The Sunday school teacher had her children draw a picture of the manger scene for Christmas week. The students all drew wonderful variations on the same basic theme: Mary and Joseph, the infant in the cradle, the animals, the shepherds, the wise men. Something about little Wayne's drawing baffled her, though.

"What's that large box in front of everyone, with the lines coming out of the top?" she asked.

"That's their television set," Wayne said proudly.

"Mom, are there animals in heaven?"

"What kinds of animals?"

"Regular animals, like cows and bees."

"I'm not sure about that. I doubt they'll be *necessary* in heaven."

"Then where are we going to get enough milk and honey for everybody?"

"Dad, are people really made of dust, like the Bible says?"

"In a sense, yes."

"And we're all going to return to dust when our bodies die."

"Certainly."

"Well, we better stay outa the closet. Somebody's either coming or going in there, right now."

A new employee was being shown the ropes at the office.

"What our management looks for more than anything else," said the supervisor, "is for everyone here to be methodical. You can get by with a few deficiencies in other regards, but you absolutely *must* be methodical."

The newcomer, stunned, said, "Well, I may as well turn in my resignation right now."

"But you haven't even started work!"

"No, and I don't plan to. I've been a deep-water Baptist all my life, and I don't see any good reason to become a Methodical at this point in time."

A church is an excellent place to go for faithlifts.

COLLEGE

Father: "You're telling me your entire class got an A in philosophy? How?"

Daughter: "We proved the professor didn't exist. What could she do?"

The parents of a first-year college student received this note from their child:

Dear Mom & Dad,
    Univer$ity life i$ $o wonderful! Cla$$e$ are intere$ting, cla$$mate$ are the be$t. The only thing I need right now i$ a little ca$h.
                                        Love,
                                        Dabney

After deliberating, they drafted an appropriate response:

Dear Dabney,
    NOt much is happening here on the NOrth side of town since you left for NOrthwestern U. See you at Thanksgiving in NOvember? Loved your letter. Write aNOther one when you have time. Have to go NOw.
                                        Love,
                                        Mom & Dad

"I'll never finish that book report," moaned the English major. "It's due tomorrow, and I've read only two chapters."

"No sweat," said the roommate. "Those new literary briefs at the campus bookshop are great. Scan over them for twenty minutes, and half your work is done!"

"Gee, thanks! I'll buy two copies, then!"

A professor was turned down on his application to a new college post. "Not enough published work," said the dean. "You have only one book to your credit."

"Are you aware that God Himself has only one book to His credit?"

"Then He needn't apply here."

COMPUTERS

Two information services managers were complaining about their work.

"If our computers could think for themselves, my problems would be over," said one.

"If my technical staff could think for themselves, so would mine," said the other.

What's the first symptom a computer is getting old?
Memory problems.

A sales clerk in an electronics store noticed a customer staring at a display unit. The display was a voice-activated computer with a built-in microphone.

The clerk mosied over and whispered to the baffled customer, "It's a voice computer. You simply speak to it, as you would to a person. The first thing it needs to know, in order to begin operating, is your name."

The customer watched the clerk walk away, then leaned near the computer and whispered, "My name's Sam Smith. What's your name?"

While trying to run four different programs in memory and juggle data between them, a typist saw this error message appear onscreen: FORGET IT. YOU'RE ASKING TOO MUCH.

Another computer operator received this error message: THREE THINGS IN LIFE ARE GUARANTEED: TAXES, DEATH, AND COMPUTER CRASHES. GUESS WHICH ONE JUST HAPPENED.

"I'll just never be able to use computers," whined Grant. "I don't think I have the basic aptitude for them."

"But they're so easy to use these days," said Cameron. "A lot of times, the only thing you have to do to answer the computer's prompts is 'PRESS ANY KEY.'"

"Yeah, that's one of my problems. I've never been able to find the 'ANY' key."

What's a tall computer's worst health fear?
The slipped disk.

COWBOYS

Two aged wranglers were relaxing in the bunkhouse, yearning for the old times.

"I hate all this automobile traffic around here," one said. "There are too many cars and trucks on the road for safety, these days."

"Well, one good thing's come of it," said his partner.

"And just what, exactly, might that be?"

"Not nearly as many rustlers to track down."

Why do cowboys need two spurs? Are they afraid one side of the horse might take off galloping by itself?

Dude: "What's the name of this ranch?"

Rancher: "Why, it's the Bar-B Double-D Crooked-T Circle-M."

Dude: "Kinda hard to remember all that, ain't it?"

Rancher: "I s'pose so."

Dude: "Where are all the cows?"

Rancher: "Can't keep any. One look at that branding iron, and they're *gone!*"

CRIME

The governor was visiting the state penitentiary and chatting with a few of the inmates as he walked down a corridor of cells.

"What are you here for?" he asked one prisoner.

"I was framed. They convicted me of embezzlement, but it was my business partner who plotted the whole thing and got all the money."

"And what about you?" he asked another.

"Armed robbery—but it was a case of mistaken identity. Some of the witnesses picked me out of a lineup, but I swear the real robber was somebody who just happened to look like me."

One by one, the inmates he spoke to declared their innocence—until he came to the last man on the cell block. "Perjury," the man answered. "I did it, sure enough. I made a terrible mistake, and now I'm paying for it, fair and square."

The governor turned to the warden and ordered the man released immediately.

"But why?" the warden asked, amazed.

"Because he's a crook," the governor said loudly. "He admits it. He's a bad example, contaminating the minds of this whole block of innocent men, and he needs to be removed."

"The prosecutor says she can produce five witnesses who saw you running from the bank with the money bags," a defense lawyer confided to a suspect.

"That's nothing," said the suspect. "I can produce five hundred witnesses who didn't see me running from the bank."

Judge, to repeat offender: "What are you charged with this time, Mr. Smith?"
Smith: "I was just trying to get my Christmas shopping done early."
Police officer: "Yes—before the store opened, Your Honor."

Several security guards were scratching their heads in the aftermath of a bank robbery.

"But how could they have gotten away?" one wondered aloud. "We had all the exits guarded."

"I think they must have gone out the entrance," suggested another.

"That'll be ten years," the judge announced harshly at the conclusion of a robbery trial. "Does the defendant have anything more to say to the court?"

"Your Honor," the defendant pleaded, "there's no way I could've been the guy who robbed that bank. I swear I was all the way across town holding up a convenience store at exactly the same moment the bank was being heisted."

"Make that twenty years," said the judge.

A poor bookseller walked through Central Park on his way home each evening. One Monday, a masked man jumped from behind a tree. "Give me your money!"

"I have no money. I'm just a poor bookseller. Here's my wallet; see for yourself."

Finding the wallet and the victim's pockets all empty, the bandit grumbled and ran off into the darkening shrubbery.

The next Monday, the same bandit accosted the bookseller. "Give me your money!" Again, he made off without a dime.

This happened each Monday evening for a month. Finally, the bookseller said to him, "Look, you recognize me. You know I'm only a poor bookseller, and I don't carry any money at all. Why do you waste your time and risk getting caught every Monday?"

The robber replied, "I'm still practicing, and you don't seem to mind too much."

After weeks of agonizing physical training, police academy cadets still hadn't been admitted to the firing range.

"I don't get it," huffed one trainee to another as they pounded out yet another five-mile jog.

"What do you mean?"

"We still don't know how to protect people and property, but we're getting real good at running away."

Judge: "You're accused of stealing a typewriter. How do you plead?"

Defendant: "I'm innocent, Your Honor. That whole thing was a mistake."

Judge: "How so?"

Defendant: "I thought it was the cash register."

A new prisoner was shown to a cell he was to share with a crusty old lifer.

"How long's your sentence?" was the veteran's first question.

"Well, thirty years—but I'm up for parole in ten," said the rookie.

"Then I get the bunk nearest the door," said the vet. "My parole comes up in only six years."

The first morning of a general sessions court term brought scores of defendants, police officers, prospective jurors, and lawyers into the courtroom. The hubbub was so impossible that the presiding judge cracked her gavel. "I'll throw out the next person who makes a sound!"

To which a chorus of criminals and their defense lawyers roared, "Hurrah!"

DATING

On their third date, the guy was astounded that the girl of his dreams actually accepted his hasty proposal of marriage.

"Gee, I. . .I'm so flattered," he stammered. "I know I certainly don't deserve you. I don't have much money, and I realize I'm not the greatest-looking fellow around, either."

"Oh, don't worry about all that," she said with a wave of her hand. "You'll be away at work twelve or fourteen hours every day."

A girl was thrilled to be invited out to dinner by the high school football star. She found it difficult to engage him in intellectual conversation, however.

"Do you enjoy reading Charles Dickens?" she ventured.

"Sure. I buy every new book he comes out with."

DEFINITIONS

ABASH: a high school graduation party.

ACCOUNT: a countess's husband.

ACUPUNCTURIST: a Chinese doctor who quietly does his jab.

ALARM CLOCK: a machine invented to scare the daylights into you.

ALIMONY: the place where Crockett, Bowie, Travis, and about 180 other guys died fighting for Texas's independence.

ANTIQUE: an item your grandparents bought, your parents got rid of, and you're buying again.

ARGUMENT: a fight over who can get in the last word first.

BARGAIN: something that's so cheap you can't resist it, even though you can't use it and don't really want it.

BARIUM: what we do to most people when they die.

BETA TESTER: anyone who uses any computer program.

BLACKOUT: an abnormality of electrical power that turns a $2,000 computer system into so many paperweights.

BUSINESS MEETING: a time for people to talk about what they're supposed to be doing.

CATALOGS: rails used to construct cow fences.

CONFIDENCE: the human quality that comes before experience.

COURTESY: the art of yawning with your mouth closed.

DERANGE: land where de buffalo roam.

DISCRETION: the art of being wiser than anyone while letting no one know it.

ENCORES: songs performers have to sing until they finally get one right.

ETC.: an abbreviation used to make people think you have additional information.

EXPERIENCE: something you've acquired after it's too late to do you much good.

EXPERT: someone who knows the answers—assuming you ask the right questions.

EXPIRATION: the process of not breathing.

FURLOUGH: snore duty.

GOBLET: a young turkey.

GOSSIPERS: people who believe anything they overhear.

GRADUATE SCHOOL: the approximate point at which a university student ceases dependency on parents and commences dependency on spouse.

HEADACHE: a pain reliever deficiency.

HOSPITAL: the place to wind up people who are run down.

IMPORT: an inland seaport.

IMPOSSIBILITY: something no one can do until someone does it.

INCOME TAX: the cause of spring fever.

KNOW-IT-ALL: a person who knows everything there is to know about nothing.

LOVE: what happens when imagination overpowers common sense.

LOW MILEAGE: what you get when your car won't start.

MIDDLE AGE: when you're sitting home alone on Friday night, and you hope the phone doesn't ring.

MISER: a person who lives poor and dies rich.

MISNOMER: the correct word for an incorrect word.

MONEY: a device by which parents stay in touch with their college children.

MUNDANE: the day after a wonderful weekend.

NAIL: what amateur carpenters replace with their thumb while the hammer is in motion.

NERVOUS DISORDER: a hereditary condition parents inherit from their teenage children.

NEWSCAST: one place where good rarely triumphs over evil.

NOTHING: the presence of absence.

NUCLEAR SCIENTIST: a professional with a lot of ions in the fire.

OPPORTUNIST: a mail carrier who enjoys the view when treed by a dog.

OPPORTUNITY: something that knocks but doesn't turn the door handle.

OPTIMIST: someone blithely ignorant of how serious a crisis really is.

ORTHODONTIST: a doctor who braces children and straps parents.

OXYGEN: a little-used form of the word "ox."

PESSIMIST: a former optimist.

PHOENICIA: an ancient Mediterranean seaport remembered for its dearth of telephone communication.

PHONETIC: an example of a word that isn't spelled the way it sounds.

PRACTICAL NURSE: a nurse who marries a wealthy patient.

QUALITY CONTROL: corporate term for "nagging."

QUICKSILVER: what the Lone Ranger says when he needs to go fast.

ROME: what buffalo do.

SCOREKEEPER: the symphony orchestra's librarian.

SHANGHAI: opposite of Shanglow.

SPICE: plural of spouse.

STEERING COMMITTEE: a panel of individuals who aren't capable of driving by themselves.

SUBORDINATE CLAUSE: the grammatically correct term for Santa Claus's assistant.

TACT: the knack for knowing exactly what not to say.

TEAMWORK: getting a group of individuals to do what one person tells them to.

TIME: the component of life that keeps everything bad from happening to you all at once.

TRAGIC OPERA: a musical-theatrical performance in which most of the characters sing, then die.

UNBREAKABLE: an adjective used to describe many toys—with the implied disclaimer that any warranties are voided where children are present.

UPWARD ADJUSTMENT: a price increase.

VEGETARIAN: a person who refuses to eat meat in public.

VENICE: one of the planets.

WAKE-UP CALL: the issue of mind over mattress.

WASTEBASKET: a receptacle near which trash is tossed.

WIDE RECEIVER: a twelve-foot TV antenna.

YACHT: a floating credit liability.

DiETING

"Wilma will never make much progress with her diet."

"Why do you think not?"

"She has some bizarre ideas about calorie counting. For example, she thinks if you have a slice of chocolate cake with a cup of low-calorie instant cocoa, they cancel out each other."

A couple were enjoying a dinner party at the home of friends. Near the end of the meal, the wife slapped her husband's arm.

"That's the third time you've gone for dessert," she said. "The hostess must think you're an absolute pig."

"I doubt that," the husband said. "I've been telling her it's for you."

"I'm starting a new diet the doctor prescribed."

"What inspired that?"

"I'm thick and tired of being thick and tired."

Jeff: Why are you so eager to meet the right woman, settle down, and get married?

Mike: So I can stop dieting.

"I thought you said you were counting calories," remarked Mrs. Bowker, scowling as her friend Mrs. Halburton enjoyed her second chocolate shake at the ice cream shop.

"I am indeed," said Mrs. Halburton between slurps. "So far today, this makes 7,750."

"Have you heard about the amazing new pasta diet?"

"No. What's involved?"

"It's so simple! You simply learn to walk pasta da refrigerator without stopping, and pasta da cookie jar, and pasta da cupboard. . . ."

DOCTORS & PATIENTS

A particular patient called on his doctor frequently, usually with imaginary ailments.

"Doc, you gotta help me," he said. "I'm really worried this time. This is serious."

"Okay, Phil. What seems to be the problem?"

"I think I'm becoming a hypochondriac."

Doctor: "That's a horrible gash on your skull. What happened?"

Child: "My sister hit me with some tomatoes."

Doctor: "That's incredible. I've never seen a tomato cut before."

Child: "Well, these were in a can."

A young man brought his wife to a small town doctor's office in an emergency. The nurses escorted the woman to the examination area, and the husband anxiously took a seat in the lobby.

For the next few minutes, he could hear the doctor bark an unsettling string of orders to the staff. First it was "Screwdriver!" Then "Knife!" Then "Pliers!"

When he heard "Sledge hammer!" the young man could bear the tension no longer. He burst into the examination room and shrieked, "Doctor, what's *wrong* with her?"

"We have no idea," the doctor said. "Right now, we're still trying to open the medicine cabinet."

The doctor was amazed at the health and durability of Mrs. Sedgefield, age ninety-two. "What's your secret to long life and health?" he asked her.

"Honey and mathematics."

"What do you mean, honey and mathematics?"

"Every morning since I was a baby, I've had a spoonful of honey. If you take that every day, and then multiply it by 33,580 days, you'll live to be ninety-two, just like me."

"I've had horrible indigestion for the past two days," a patient said.

"And what have you been doing for it?" asked the doctor.

"Taking an antacid twice a day and drinking nothing but milk," said the patient.

"Good—exactly what I would have suggested myself. That'll be $50."

Doctor: "So you haven't been able to sleep well?"
Patient: "I sleep fine during the night, but during my afternoon naps, I just can't keep my eyes closed."

A doctor's receptionist answered the phone and was screamed at by an excited man at the other end of the line.

"My wife's in labor!" he yelled. "I think she's going to deliver any minute now."

"Please calm down," the receptionist said. "Try to relax and give me some basic information. Is this her first child?"

"No, no! I'm her husband!"

"Doc, it's my husband!" shrieked a woman into the phone. "I served lasagna for dinner last night, and this morning he's turned all blue!"

"Sing him a song," suggested the doctor. "Tell him a joke."

Emergency Room Receptionist: "What's the problem?"
Incoming Patient: "These pains in my sides and back. I feel like I have double pneumonia."
Receptionist: "We have only single beds. Which side would you like treated?"

An auto mechanic in the hospital was chatting nervously with his surgeon while being prepped for an operation. "Sometimes I wish I'd gone into your line of work," he told the doctor. "Everything you doctors do is so cut and dried and tidy. With me, I spend half a day taking an engine apart and putting it back together, and it seems I always have a couple of parts left over."

"Yes," said the surgeon. "I know the feeling."

A pharmacist was squinting and holding the prescription slip up to the light. Finally, she took up a magnifier in a futile effort to read it.

"We don't think too highly of this particular doctor," she told the customer, "but there's one thing he obviously can do better than anyone else on the planet."

"What's that?"

"Read his own handwriting."

Doctor: "What seems to be the problem with little Micah today?"
Panicked Parent: "We think he swallowed a bullet!"
Doctor: "For heaven's sake, stop pointing him at me!"

Doctor: "How are you feeling?"
Patient: "I feel a whole lot more like I do now than I did a little while ago."

Patient: "Doc, what do you recommend for an insomniac like me?"
Doctor: "A good night's sleep."

Doctor: "What seems to be the problem?"
Patient's wife: "It's my husband. He's swallowed my fountain pen."
Doctor: "That's serious. Have you done anything about it?"
Patient's wife: "Yes, I've made him buy me a new one."

Doctors in the emergency room examined the incoming patient, a hit-and-run victim, with concern. Several broken ribs, a fractured femur, and various other internal and external injuries indicated tedious surgical procedures were in order. It was amazing the patient was momentarily conscious.

"Are you allergic to anything?" one doctor asked.
"Yes," she replied weakly.
"What's that?"
"Oncoming trucks."

DRIVERS

A driving student was poring through the handbook just before taking the written exam. Suddenly, he got up and hurried from the training room.

"Hey, where are you going?" the instructor demanded.

"I'm outa here, Man. Gotta phone my parents, like, right now!"

"What's the matter? Don't you want to earn your driver's license?"

"Doesn't matter. First thing we have to do is move, and I mean *today!*"

"Move? You mean move your family?"

"Yep. Lock, stock, and motorcycle. Find a new house."

"What on earth for?"

"It says in that book that 90 percent of all traffic fatalities in the United States occur within five miles of home."

"I clocked you doing ninety-six miles an hour, Buddy. Something wrong?"

"No, Officer, nothing's actually wrong. I'd simply forgotten to plug in my radar detector."

Patrol Officer: "Didn't you see the sixty-five-mile-per-hour speed limit signs?"

Driver: "I thought those were only suggestions."

Some teenage friends were marveling at the scene of an accident where one of them miraculously had walked away from the mishap without a scratch the night before.

"Wow, that was some smash-up," said one.

"Totaled the car," said another.

"How'd it happen?" asked a third.

The victim pointed to a tilted telephone pole. "See that?"

"Yeah."

"I didn't."

"My dad must be a pretty bad driver," said Brad.

"What do you mean?" asked Bret.

"I was with him when he got pulled for speeding yesterday. The officer recognized him and wrote him out a season ticket."

A stranger drove to a halt beside a pedestrian in a tiny, remote village. Lost and in a hurry, the driver had no desire to engage in conversation with the locals; he only wanted quick directions.

"Hey, Idiot," he snapped. "Can you tell me how to get to Portland?"

"Yes," the villager said, before turning to cross the street and disappear inside a shop door.

A team of paramedics loaded a dazed auto accident victim into the ambulance.

"I don't understand it," the stunned patient moaned. "I'm sure I had the right-of-way."

"Yes," said a medic, "but the other driver had the eighteen-wheeler."

A patrol officer chased down a speeder after a thirty-mile adventure on the interstate—only after the speeder had run out of gas.

"Congratulations," said the officer sarcastically. "You hit 163 miles per hour. I didn't think a little subcompact like that could give me such a run."

"And congratulations to you. I didn't think you could keep up."

A highway patrolman stopped a car for flagrantly speeding on I-95.

"Don't you know the speed limit?" he asked.

"Sure. It's ninety-five. It's posted every few miles."

"That's the highway number, not the speed limit."

"I realized it was kinda fast—but I figured it was the government's way of letting people make up for lost time."

"Lost time? What do you mean?"

"Well, if those aren't speed limit signs, then I guess I spent the first half of the day on Interstate 20."

"I'm only giving you a warning," said the policeman, handing a form to a beautiful but distressed-looking young woman he'd stopped for speeding.

"Oh, thank you so much, Officer!" she said, folding the warning ticket neatly into her purse. "I collect these."

ECONOMICS

A young couple were about to buy an electric grill and put it on their credit card. They debated whether to select the economy model or the deluxe unit that had every imaginable convenience.

"Ah, let's go ahead and get the big one," said the husband.

"Yeah," said his wife. "It won't really cost us any more. We'll just have to pay a little longer."

Many investors require a stockbroker one day and a pawnbroker the next.

Have you heard about the hot new credit plan? You put 100 percent down and have no monthly payments!

When you need to borrow money, borrow it from a pessimist. Pessimists don't expect it to be returned.

Money talks, but it has a one-word vocabulary: *Good-bye*.

A woman was extremely impressed with a gold watch in a jewelry shop. "You say this is only $29.95," she remarked to the jeweler. "There must be something wrong with it."

"No, Madam. It's simply marked down to a dollar above cost."

"You're telling me you paid only $29 for it yourself?"

"That's correct, Madam."

"Nonsense. If that's true, how could you possibly make a living?"

"You forget, Madam, this is also a repair shop."

Did you ever wonder why hamburger buns come eight to a package—when hamburger patties come in packages of five or ten?

After successfully getting their big line items approved in the congressional spending package, two lobbyists were celebrating at a Washington restaurant.

"You know," mused one, "it's a crying shame our grandchildren and great-grandchildren haven't been born yet so they can see the terrific things the government's doing with their money."

FAMiLY TiES

She: "Our problem is that we're just not communicating."
He: "I don't wanna discuss it."

A farmer's wife went into a coma at home, and he summoned the doctor.

"She's gone," said the doc after examining the woman. "I'm very sorry. I'll call the funeral home for you."

The morticians carried the body down the porch steps and started to round the corner of the house into the driveway when the lead bearer suddenly lurched to avoid a holly bush, lost his balance, and dropped his end of the stretcher. The jolt brought the woman back to consciousness. In a week, she'd made a full recovery and was back at the farm.

Several years later she again went into a coma. This time, the doctor sadly assured her husband she was unquestionably dead.

The undertakers were summoned. As the stretcher bearers inched down the steps and headed for the driveway with the corpse, the farmer cautioned, "Watch out for that holly bush."

When he went to visit his cousin in the big city, Farmer Dan was amazed at the dozens of cats loitering around the apartment complex. "Why don't you shoo 'em?" he asked his cousin.

"Here in town, we let the cats go barefoot."

A man died and, as he'd requested, was cremated. But he didn't specify what was to be done with the ashes. They ended up in an hourglass in his widow's kitchen cabinet.

"Why do you keep him there?" a friend asked.

"Well, he never was good for much when he was alive. At least now I can put him to work timing the casseroles."

The new bride had spent two hours preparing her first breakfast. She sat at the table, eagerly watching as her husband slowly savored each forkful.

"How was it, Honey?" she asked when he'd finished.

"Well," he began thoughtfully, wiping his lips, "you probably could have beaten the eggshells a little longer. But on the whole, it was a good start."

A beloved matron of the town was dying. Her family stood by, reflecting on her many wonderful qualities.

"She was the perfect mother," said one grown daughter. "Always there, always caring, always loving—but not to be disobeyed."

"She was the same to the whole community," said a son. "Everyone in town, I believe, regarded her as if she were their own mother."

"She sure knew how to cook!" chirped a grandson, sending a ripple of subdued chuckles through the morose gathering.

"And she was always the first to volunteer," added her minister.

The old woman turned her head on the pillow to face them. She moaned, "Motherhood. Cooking. Volunteering. Not one comment about how wonderfully modest I am."

A woman was deeply depressed after her husband's death—until the insurance agent appeared in a few weeks with a $300,000 benefit check.

"I do believe," she confided to a friend, "I'd give $5,000 to have him back."

Grandson: "Grandma, how many brothers and sisters did you have?"

Grandma: "Eleven brothers and eight sisters."

Grandson: "Wow! I bet yours was the biggest family in the whole town."

Grandma: "Yes. I expect that's why they built the new school next to our house."

At 3:00 in the morning, a young wife shook her husband awake.

"What is it?" he asked groggily.

"The baby," she reminded him.

The husband sat up and listened a full minute. "But I don't hear her crying," he protested.

"I know. It's your turn to go see why not."

Two cousins were having a friendly chat when one blurted, out of the blue, "Man, I need to borrow $100 from somebody by the end of the week."

"Really?"

"I sure do. Don't know who to turn to, either."

"I'm very glad to hear that. It sounded for a moment like you were gonna turn to me."

Mother was amused when she heard her six-year-old son whining to a friend: "I don't get it. My sister insists she has three brothers. But I'm in the same family, and I count only two brothers. . . ."

Smith: "I understand the Family Court social worker was at your house asking questions the other day."

Jones: "Yeah, my son was telling everyone at school he came from a broken home."

Smith: "Broken home? I thought you and Angie were happily married."

Jones: "We are. But the cement's coming loose between the blocks in our basement."

A young couple were discussing what to name their newborn son.

"I really like the name Ryan," the mother said.

"Nah," said her husband. "Every Tom, Dick, and Harry these days is called Ryan."

"Now, Charles, come give your old aunt a kiss before she goes," Aunt Meg said, putting on her gloves.

Charles shook his head.

"Come, now, Charles." She took a quarter from her purse and smiled. "I'll give you this if you'll just give me one little kiss on the cheek, like a good boy."

"Nah," Charles said. "Mom gives me that much just for eating brussels sprouts."

Al: "You sure seem unhappy."

Hal: "Yep. Living with my mother-in-law is really stressful. She's constantly fussing at both me and my wife."

Al: "Well, if worse comes to worst, you may have to ask her to move out."

Hal: "I don't think we can do that. It's her house."

A man was lounging in the living room, reading a magazine, when his wife crowded in the front door with bulging bags from a mall.

"I thought you were only going window shopping," he teased.

"That's right. I have the new curtains for the kitchen windows —and a matching bread box, can opener, cutlery set, spice rack. . ."

Mr. Brown was seen each weekday morning peddling a bicycle to the shuttle stop, briefcase under his arm. His wife ran after him, perspiring heavily and gasping for breath.

One day a neighbor confronted Brown with his thoughtless behavior. "Why is it you ride the bicycle, and she has to run?"

"She doesn't own a bike," was the offhanded reply.

Mrs. Wade was trying to be tactful with her friend Mrs. Griffin. "Now that your son George has turned thirty, don't you think it's time he decided what to do with his life?"

"Oh, he's at a very difficult age," Mrs. Griffin said.

"What do you mean?"

"Why, he's simply caught in limbo: too old to live at home with us but too young to draw Social Security."

FARM & GARDEN

Two farmers were commiserating about the long drought.

"It's so dry now, my pond water's about gone."

"Mine, too. And I hear over in Branchville, the Baptist church has gone to sprinkling, and the Methodists are wringing cactus juice onto a handkerchief."

A farm is a place where you can get rich overnight, assuming you strike oil.

A school class was on a field trip to the farm.

"Look, look!" cried a student, pointing. "There's a little cow with no horns! All the other cows have horns. Why doesn't this one?"

The farmer puffed his pipe and drawled an explanation. "There are a lot of reasons some cows don't have horns," he said. "It might depend on the breed; some cattle breeds are horned and some aren't. Or it could be the cow's age; some don't grow horns until they're adults. And in some cases, cows that once had horns have lost them in collisions, or their owners have removed them for one reason or another.

"But in the case of this young cow here, it doesn't have horns because it's a colt."

"I want to start a garden, but my yard's a little problematic," a customer told the proprietor at the yard and garden center. "I get blazing afternoon sunshine for about two hours, but otherwise it's all shade."

"What kind of soil?" asked the proprietor.

"Hard clay, lot of rocks. What do you recommend I plant?"

"Hmmm," mused the store owner. "Why don't you look down Aisle B? We've got a big new supply of birdbaths and flagpoles. . . ."

A farmer chided his teenage grandson, "Your generation has gotten lazy. When I was fifteen, I thought nothing of getting up at daybreak to milk the cows."

"I don't think much of it, either," said the youth.

The chicken yard was thrown into a clucking fright when farm boys at play accidentally kicked a football near the coop. After the ball had been retrieved and the flock had calmed down, one hen turned to another. "Now *that*," she said, "was what I call an *egg*."

A stranger frantically ran up to a farmer's door, pounded his fist, and demanded, "Where's the nearest railroad station, and what time's the next train to the city?"

The farmer thought a moment. "Cut through my back hayfield, and you ought to reach the crossroads station in time for the 5:40. Actually, if my bull spots you, I expect you'll make the 5:15."

"You know," said the farmer to his wife, "with all the additives they're putting in our milk these days, don't you reckon it makes old Bessie feel right deficient?"

A visitor to a farm was astounded to see brown bundles of feathers zooming around the barnyard so fast they couldn't be seen clearly. "What in the world are those things?" he asked, somewhat alarmed.

"Those are my four-legged chickens," the farmer said. "I've been breedin' 'em. Quick, ain't they?"

"Yes, but why do you want four-legged chickens?"

" 'Cause me and my wife and our two boys all like the drumstick. When we have fried chicken, there'll be a leg for each of us."

"Does it taste like normal fried chicken?"

"Don't know, yet. We haven't been able to catch one."

Farmer Tanner rang up a neighbor on the telephone. "My best milking cow has a fever," he said. "How did you treat your ol' Bessie when she got sick last winter?"

"Well, I made up a mixture of half cod liver oil and half turpentine and put it in with her food once a day for four days."

"Thanks. I'll try it."

Farmer Tanner hung up the phone and proceeded to treat his cow. Shockingly, after four days of the medicine compound, the cow died.

He rang up his neighbor again. "Hey, I did exactly what you said with the cod liver oil and turpentine mixture, but my cow just died."

"Yep. So did ol' Bessie."

Farmer Brown: "Did you lose much in that last tornado?"
Farmer Jones: "Lost the henhouse and all the chickens. But that was all right—I ended up with three new cows and somebody's pickup truck."

Two farmers were in a bragging match about their produce.

"The eggs I get from my hens," said one, "are so big it takes just one to make a cake."

"Well, the ones I get are so big it takes just ten to make a dozen."

FiSHING

"I promised my wife I'd turn over a new leaf," Earl said. "From now on, I'm gonna fish in moderation."

A man and his wife were in a boat on a lake. While the man fished, his wife read a book, shading herself with an umbrella.

The game warden motored up. "Don't you know this is a private lake?" the warden told the man. "It would be breaking the law to take any fish from here."

"Actually, Officer," the wife intervened, "for him, it would be miraculous."

Angler's motto: "I only fish on days that end in 'y.' "

FOOTBALL

Social Studies Teacher: "Tony, what can you tell us about Houston, Texas?"
Tony: "It was the birthplace of the Tennessee Oilers."

"The X-ray shows a small spot under your kneecap, but it's probably just scar tissue," the doctor told the college quarterback. "I'm not very concerned about it."

The quarterback was not assured. "If it was your knee," he retorted, "I wouldn't be very concerned, either."

Head Coach: "That George is a slacker. He's so slow my grandmother could run him down."
Assistant Coach: "Well, there's one thing he does fast. Real fast. Faster'n anybody else on the team."
Head Coach: "What's that?"
Assistant Coach: "Get tired."

GROWNUPS

"Dad, there's something I've gotta tell you," Shane said, following his father inside the bait shop.

"Not, now, Son. I have to select our fish bait."

Later, entering the convenience store, Shane tried again. "Hey, Dad—"

"Hold on, Son. I have to grab some lunch for our fishing trip."

At the gas station, dad was filling the boat tank when Shane began, "Dad, there's something you really need to know. . . ."

"Just wait, Son. I need to pay for this gas so we can hit the road."

An hour later, as they sat on the pond bank catching fish, the father remembered his son's nagging. "What was it you were trying to tell me awhile ago?" he asked.

"Oh, not much. Just that your fly is open."

"Mom, why do you put on all that makeup before you go to bed?" a child asked, watching her mother apply the nightly ritual.

"It's not really makeup," her mother explained. "It's mostly a variety of creams to protect my skin and make me feel better after a long day. This one is for wrinkles, for example. And this hand lotion is great for my joints. And this facial cream gives me a healthy, pink color."

"I'm surprised they don't leave you black and blue all over."

"Why do you say that?"

"They make you so greasy, you must slip out of bed a lot and fall on the floor."

A five year old came into the kitchen and asked, "Mommy, can I have a slice of strawberry pie?"

"Now, Randall," his mother corrected, "you don't say 'can I have.' You say 'may I have.' "

"Okay. May I have a slice of strawberry pie?"

"And what do you say at the end?"

"Oh—may I have a slice of strawberry pie, please?"

"No, dear. We'll be having dinner in less than an hour."

"Dad, which do you think is America's worst problem: ignorance or apathy?"

"Don't know. Don't really care, either."

"But I don't wanna help Billy with his homework," Father complained to Mother. "It's boring, and he shouldn't need help, anyway. He's simply not thinking for himself. He's getting someone else to do his thinking for him."

"Now, Honey, you go in there and help him while you can," Mother replied. "You know he'll soon be a third-grader."

"Mom, Dad just hit his thumb with a hammer."

"Oh, dear. What did he say?"

"You wouldn't want me to repeat any bad words, would you, Mom?"

"Certainly not."

"Well, then, he didn't say anything."

HiLLBiLLiES &
OLD-TiMERS

"I hear old Ebenezer Todd died the other day up in Jonesville," said an old-timer, playing checkers at the country store.

"Yeah, they say he died of a head injury."

"Head injury? It must've taken a powerful wallop to do in that tough old coot."

"No, wasn't much more'n a scratch, from what I hear. He was startin' to come around, but then his wife came along and tied a tourniquet around his neck."

A stranger walked inside the community store at a remote village. "Where's the movie theater?" he asked.

"We don't have one," the clerk replied.

"What about a golf course?"

"We don't play golf."

"Well, where's your local baseball diamond? Surely you have baseball."

"Nope."

"Then what do you do for fun around here? Where do you people play video games?"

"Same place we play baseball and golf and watch movies."

The city woman was driving a secondary route through the mountains at night. She hadn't seen a town for miles, and her gas gauge was almost on empty. Finally, she came to a crossroads community with a few houses. A ramshackle country store had a light on and a single, antiquated gas pump in front. Happily, the storekeeper assured her that the pump still worked.

"This sure is a tiny village," the woman said as he topped off her tank. "What on earth do you do for a living around here?"

"We charge $10 a gallon for gas," he drawled.

Ma: "I think Adam and Eve must have been hillbillies, just like us."

Pa: "What makes you say that?"

Ma: "Didn't have a fancy house. Didn't drive a car. Didn't go to college. Didn't have any money—but as far as they were concerned, life was just like paradise."

A salesman was trying to strike up a conversation with a wily, tight-lipped mountaineer. "Have you lived all your life in these parts?" he tried.

"Not yet," was the sour reply.

HISTORY

"Who invented the bow and arrow?" asked the teacher.

"Cavemen!" cried Gary enthusiastically.

"Cavemen? And what do you suppose prompted cavemen to come up with the bow and arrow?"

"Er. . .somebody kept stealing the wheel?"

"What would be your definition of 'liberty'?" asked the civics teacher.

"That was the first choice of Patrick Henry."

"What was the principal occupation of the ancient Babylonians?" a college history student was asked.

"Dying, I believe."

"What do you think was the most important invention in all of history?" the teacher asked his class.

"The automobile," said one student.

"The airplane," said another.

"The nuclear submarine," said the third.

"The credit card," said the fourth.

History Teacher: "Who was the most famous Egyptian in history?"
Student: "The Mummy."

"Can you give us an example of an absolute monarchy?" the teacher asked.

"France, during the colonial period."

"And we know that absolute monarchies present lots of difficulties for the common people, don't we?"

"Yeah, but they sure are cool for the monarch."

HUMAN NATURE

Three mice lugged their prize of cheese out to the shade tree to enjoy a picnic lunch. Suddenly, a dark cloud came up, and it began raining heavily.

"We need an umbrella," said one. "Who's going back to the house to get it?"

Each mouse was afraid that if it left the picnic, the other two would eat all the cheese. Finally, they resolved the question by drawing straws. The loser hesitantly disappeared into the driving rain.

The two other mice eyed the cheese hungrily. But being honest critters, they refrained from indulging before their friend returned with the umbrella.

The third mouse was gone for ten minutes. Then thirty minutes. Then an hour.

"Something's happened," said one of the waiting mice. "I don't think our friend's coming back today. We may as well dig into the cheese."

"I agree," said the other.

Just then the third mouse squeaked from behind the tree, "Touch that cheese, and I won't go for the umbrella!"

Mick: "Can you keep a secret?"
Rick: "Sure. Of course, I can't vouch for the prudence of the people I tell it to."

Gizmo: "Are you superstitious?"
Dave: "*Shh!* It's bad luck to be superstitious."

A group of detectives was lounging around the police station.

"I can't believe it," said one. "We haven't had a thing to investigate for the past two days. No shootings, no robberies, no embezzlements, no nothing."

"Just give folks a little time," said a partner.

Harold: "My mom said it's only a coincidence that you and I have the same last name, because we're not related. Do you know what the word 'coincidence' means?"
George: "Nah, I was about to ask you what it means."

"Old Mr. Clancy sure is grumpy."

"What makes you think so?"

"If you pay him a compliment, he doesn't trust you. If you don't pay him regular compliments, he doesn't like you at all."

Mother: "Jack, you're always procrastinating. You *must* change."
Jack: "Sure, Mom. I'll change, I promise. I'll start Monday."

HUNTiNG

A man attired in camouflage entered a butcher shop. "Can you sell me a couple of undressed ducks?" he asked.

"Well, no. We have no fresh ducks at the moment. I can sell you a nice selection of poultry broilers, though."

"Chickens!" the customer scoffed. "No way. I can't go home and tell my wife I bagged a couple of chickens!"

Four hunters were bragging about the merits of their favorite blue tick hounds.

"My ol' Benny goes to the store for me," said one. "Always brings me back my favorite brand of tobacco."

"My dog Suzie buys our grits at that same store," said another. "I give her a five-dollar bill, and she brings me back the change first, then returns for the bag of grits."

"I send ol' Mack there for my shotgun shells," said the third. "He knows exactly what gauge and brand I want."

The fourth hunter said nothing until he was prompted by the others to try to top their tales.

"I reckon my dog ain't much to speak of, by comparison," he allowed. "He just sits in the store all day and operates the cash register."

Two easterners were hunting in the Rocky Mountain wilderness when a huge grizzly bear sprang onto their path, reared up, and roared.

One hunter was paralyzed with fright. The other kept his presence of mind and advised calmly, "Don't move a muscle. Just stand like a statue, and the bear will get bored and go away."

"H–h–how do you know?"

"Read it in a book about the Lewis and Clark expedition."

So they stood motionless. The bear didn't go away, but instead drew closer and roared more furiously.

"I–I–I think the bear must've read that same book!" stammered the frightened hunter.

Paul: "Willie finally shot his first wild duck this morning."

Brad: "Reckon it won't be worth cookin'."

Paul: "Why not?"

Brad: "Must've been a very old duck, if it was flyin' low enough for Willie to shoot it."

KNOCK-KNOCKS

Knock-knock!
Who's there?
Osborn.
Osborn Who?
Osborn way up in the heels.

Knock-knock!
Who's there?
Virgil.
Virgil Who?
Virgil reality seems to be the hot topic of discussion these days.

Knock-knock!
Who's there?
Rufus.
Rufus Who?
Rufus smokin'. I think your house is on fire.

Knock, Knock!
Who's there?
Amaryllis.
Amaryllis Who?
Amaryllis state agent looking for property in your neighborhood.

Knock-knock!
Who's there?
Heaven.
Heaven Who?
Heaven you the courtesy to open the door and let me in?

Knock-knock!
Who's there?
Doughnut.
Doughnut Who?
Doughnut keep me waiting out here too long, please.

Knock-knock!
Who's there?
Icon.
Icon Who?
Icon operate three programs at one time on my computer.

LAWYERS & CLIENTS

A lawyer was advising a client. "Do you have written documentation that the used car dealer promised to service the car after you bought it?" the attorney asked.

"No, it was a verbal agreement."

"*Ach!* Verbal agreements aren't worth the paper they're written on."

A couple gaped at the TV as they watched their lawyer being interviewed during a newscast. The reporter wanted the attorney's comments for a local angle in a late-breaking Supreme Court decision.

"I wonder how in the world she got hold of our lawyer," the husband said, shaking his head. "I've been trying to get him to update our will for the last three weeks, and his secretary invariably says he's with clients."

"I love my profession," said the lawyer. "With each new client, it's a challenge, with a brand-new set of facts and a different solution. I never know what to do until I've studied the situation and researched the case law."

"Whereas in my profession," remarked the mortician sadly, "I know exactly what I'm going to do for all my clients before they even come through the door."

Two young attorneys fresh out of law school were sharing lunch. "I just got my first case!" one beamed excitedly.

"Oh? Who's the client?"

"Me!"

"You?!? You're representing yourself in your first case?"

"Yeah. I'm being sued."

"By whom?"

"By my dad."

"Your own *father* is suing you? What for?"

"For the $55,000 he spent sending me to law school."

A lawyer was cross-examining an elderly witness in a robbery case. He thought he'd capitalize on the probability that her eyesight left something to be desired.

"Mrs. Wilson, would you please tell us your age?"

"I'm seventy-eight years old," she said proudly.

"And have you ever worn eyeglasses?"

"I carry a pair in my purse, but I hardly ever need them."

"Is that so? Now, Mrs. Wilson, how far away from the scene of the crime were you standing?"

"I was down the street a little ways. They tell me it was sixty or seventy yards."

"Are you absolutely certain you can see things clearly at that distance?"

"I suppose so. We're 240,000 miles from the moon, and I can see that just fine on clear nights."

Lawyer: "Here's a draft of the brief I'm about to file in your bankruptcy claim. Better look it over."

Client: "I count thirty pages of solid type. You call this a *brief*?"

A man was describing to his lawyer the various damages caused by a neighbor's careless landscaping: shattered fence, poisoned shrubbery, drainage problems resulting from soil erosion, etc.

"So you want me to sue for damages?" the lawyer asked.

"No, I don't want you to damage him. I want you to sue him for repairs."

"I need a criminal lawyer," a stranger announced in a small-town barbershop. "Know where I might find one around here?"

"Well, Lawyer Blake and Lawyer Black are obvious choices. There are a couple others we suspect, if Blake and Black are both too busy to take your case."

LOGIC

Three university professors—an architectural engineer, a biologist, and a philosopher—always shared their morning break at a little bohemian coffee shop on a quiet corner facing the campus housing units. For several years, they absently noticed the comings and goings at a married students' apartment complex. In one particular apartment, they watched the resident students—a young man and his wife—return to their door together after an early morning class. Like clockwork, the couple returned, books under their arms, at precisely the same time each morning.

Reconvening after the long Christmas break one year, the professors were surprised to see the couple emerge from their apartment carrying an infant.

Reasoned the engineer: "Incorrect dimensions."

Reasoned the biologist: "No, a simple matter of reproduction."

Reasoned the philosopher: "Doesn't matter. What's relevant is that if one human being were now to enter the door, the apartment would be empty."

"Jill told me you told her I told you she was an airhead, and I told you not to tell her I told you that."

"It's her fault. I told her not to tell you I told her what you said."

"Well, don't let it happen again—and don't tell her I told you she told me."

Two commercial bankers were having lunch. One was a twenty-year veteran of the finance industry, the other a novice just out of business school. The younger was picking the other's brain for advice.

"Mr. Morton, what usually happens when a person with a lot of money but no experience goes into partnership with a person who has no money but lots of experience?"

"Either the venture will fail altogether," advised the senior, "or the partner with the experience will end up with all the money."

Two friends were discussing a mutual acquaintance.

"I don't think she's really antisocial," said one.

"Nah," said the other. "She just despises humans."

"How many officers do you have on your force?" a visiting relative asked a small-town police chief.

"Counting myself, there are three of us."

"Man, don't tell me this little nowhere of a crossroads needs three police officers!"

"If it weren't for us," responded the chief dryly, "it certainly would."

A retired volunteer was presented with an annual award at a community service banquet.

"I really don't deserve this," the honoree told the audience, "but then again, I expect I really don't deserve arthritis, either."

A very business-like paper boy knocked on the door of a house. When a woman answered, he demanded, "You haven't paid for your paper all month. Pay up right now, or you're off the route and you'll be hearing from our collection agency."

The woman looked around her yard and answered, "I've paid you every week, in much the same way you deliver my newspaper. Look. There's a payment envelope in the bushes to the left, one in the bushes to the right, one up in the gutter of the porch, and one in the hole in my living-room window."

Two archaeologists were pondering the inscription at the foot of the mummy's case. It read simply: 3 B.C.

"What can that mean?" wondered the first archaeologist.

"Hmm. Could be the license tag of the guy who ran him down."

Reluctant bather: "You're sure there are no sharks along this beach?"

Lifeguard: "Highly unlikely. They don't get along with the alligators."

A contented diner standing in line to pay at a buffet restaurant couldn't suppress a deep, joyous burp. Most of the people in hearing distance ignored him, but one man took offense.

"You belched in front of my wife," he challenged. "I think you should apologize."

"Oh, I'm so sorry. Was it her turn?"

"Daddy," a child asked, "didn't you break your nose when you were a little boy?"

"I'm afraid I did."

"Was it the same nose you have now?"

"To what do you attribute living to be ninety years old?" the TV talk show host asked the spry guest.

"Oh, it's a simple ritual I've followed for the last half century."

"Would you mind sharing it with our viewers?"

"Each morning when I wake up, I take three deep breaths, thank the good Lord I'm alive, drink the glass of orange juice my wife has waiting beside the bed, and glance at the newspaper."

"That's all?"

"Yep. If my name's not among the obituaries, I proceed to get up."

City cousin: "At our home we have hot and cold tap water."
Country cousin: "We do, too. Hot in the summer and cold in the winter."

Trisha: "Do you believe in smoking?"
Michele: "Well, I've seen it with my own eyes, several times."

Mack paid $650 for his gold watch. It was rustproof, shockproof, magneticproof, fireproof and, of course, waterproof. There was only one thing wrong with it: He lost it.

"Is it too windy for you?" asked Mr. Ogden, steering the sailboat onto the open bay.

"No," said Mrs. Ogden. "I'm just having a little trouble keeping my eyebrows on."

"Did I ever tell you about my adventures eradicating alligators from the streets of Manhattan?"

"There are no alligators on the streets of Manhattan."

"Nope. Not anymore."

Brett: "Why did you write TGIF on the tops of your shoes? Do you really need to be reminded it's Friday?"

Moe: "That doesn't stand for 'Thank Goodness It's Friday.' It stands for 'Toes Go In First.' "

A woman wrote a check at a department store.

"I'll have to ask you to identify yourself," the clerk said.

The customer took a small mirror from her handbag, looked into it keenly, and pronounced, "Yes. That's definitely me."

"Why do you always scratch yourself?"

"I'm the only one who knows where I itch."

What would life be like if there were no hypothetical situations?

Pessimist: "I'm a miserable failure. Always have been, always will be."
Optimist: "Maybe you just started at the bottom and felt comfortable there."

"Now remember," the driving instructor said to the aging student, "the overriding objective is for your license to expire before you do."

Two friends were discussing the relative merits of car models.
"I'm waiting for a car that'll last me a lifetime," said one.
"I hope to live longer than that," said the other.

Roger: "I thought I faxed you that information yesterday."
Kevin: "Nope. Never arrived."
Roger: "That's funny. I stamped it and everything. . . ."

MacDonald, an old highlander, was nonplused at his first encounter with a thermos bottle. "If ye put hot coffee in it, it keeps the coffee pipin' hot," delightedly explained his seven-year-old granddaughter. "If ye put in ice water, it keeps the water ice cold."

MacDonald shook his head. "Aye, I believe ye," he said. "But how does it know whether ye want it hot or cold? . . ."

MEDIA

News never is really news. It just happens to different people from day to day.

Why did Sylvia buy a small-screen TV?
She wanted to shorten the commercials.

A newspaper ran a blistering editorial in which it stated, "We believe half the members of city council are swindlers."

City hall and its political supporters flooded the editor's phone line for three days. Finally, a retraction was promised. It read: "We now believe half the members of city council are not swindlers."

Social studies teacher: "What did you like best about that mini-series on TV?"
Student: "The fact that it's over."

Teacher: "Why is television called a 'medium'?"
Student: "Because it's neither rare nor well-done."

What's the best thing on TV these days?
The "off" button.

Folks throughout the city knew they were in trouble when the new owners of the *Tribune* suavely altered the paper's time-honored motto to read: "ALL THE NEWS THAT'S FIT FOR US."

"What do you think of violence on TV?"
"Well, I guess without it, the newscasters wouldn't have anything interesting to report."

"How is Grace enjoying her retirement?"
"Well, she went back to work after a week."
"Oh, no! Why, she's been looking forward to retirement for years."
"That was before she saw what's on daytime television now."

What were the first words spoken after TV was invented?
"This is gonna be just another fad. . . ."

What do you get when you cross a good mystery with a good comedy?
A play that makes you roll in the aisles laughing. . .and wondering afterward why you behaved that way.

A cub reporter was dispatched to cover an earthquake scene. The devastation was extensive and horrible, with buildings crumbled, folks in shock, sporadic fires, and emergency workers racing hither and yon. Overwhelmed, the reporter waxed theological as she called in her story.

"Even God weeps tonight," she began dictating to her editor, "as He looks down at—"

"Forget the quake!" interrupted the editor. "Interview God. Is our photographer still around?"

Cliff: "Why do you watch all those soap operas on TV?"
Bev: "Because I can't see the actors' faces on the radio."

Warren: "Today's news makes me sick."
Matt: "What paper do you read?"
Warren: "*USA Today.*"
Matt: "Try *USA Yesterday.*"

MUSIC

"Cheryl is a true lover of classical music."

"I've figured that out. The 'William Tell Overture' is her favorite piece of music—and she doesn't know who the Lone Ranger is."

Two symphony critics were comparing notes after a concert.

"The conductor was fantastic," said one. "Did you observe how the very first crescendo literally filled the music hall?"

"Yes," said the other. "A substantial number of the audience removed themselves to give it room."

The pest control man arrived at a home and heard a horrendous barrage of attempted piano music coming through the front screen door. He knocked and waited. The noise didn't abate. He peered inside and could see a teenage lad savagely pounding through a lesson at the keyboard.

The pest control man knocked louder and finally got the woeful student's attention.

"Are your folks at home, Son?" he asked.

The boy menacingly banged out a couple of concluding, bizarre nonchords and glared at the visitor. "Take a wild guess."

Why do bagpipers march when they play?
To get 'way from the sound.

The story is told of a piano recital by a child prodigy. Among the audience were seated together two revered performers, one himself a pianist, the other an operatic tenor.

The child made the keys dance so gracefully that every listener in the hall was raised to heavenly heights. . .except the veteran pianist. Perceiving a coming shadow against his own preeminence, he squirmed visibly in his seat.

"It's dreadfully warm in here," he whispered, pulling at his collar.

"Not for vocalists," said the other.

What's the difference between bagpipes and a lawn mower?
You can tune a lawn mower.

They laughed when I sat down to play. . .for the piano had no bench.

A lady aboard a cruise ship was not impressed by the jazz trio in one of the shipboard restaurants. When her waiter came around, she asked, "Will they play anything I ask?"

"Of course, Madam."

"Then tell them to go play shuffleboard."

What's the difference between a bagpipe and an onion?
No one cries when you slice a bagpipe.

McLaramie: "Had a big racket at home t'other evenin'. Family above us were stompin' the floor and just ahollerin' til the wee hours o' the marnin'."
McClintock: "Kept ye awake, did it?"
McLaramie: "No, fortunately, I was up already, playin' muh bagpipes."

A great pianist once was asked by an erstwhile child prodigy for his advice on how to become the greatest pianist in history.

"My best advice," said the older man, "is to begin practicing while you are very young, learn all you can from your elders, and hopefully, by the time you've reached the end of your life, you will have attained your goal."

"But you were great before the age of twenty," the youngster protested.

"Perhaps," acknowledged his mentor. "But I never had to ask anyone's advice."

A couple were standing in the ticket line at the concert hall when the husband remarked, "I wish we'd brought along our piano bench."

"What in the world for?"

"Because the tickets are inside the seat."

What's the best way to tune a tuba?

With a hack saw.

A community chorus conductor came home from the first rehearsal in a sour temper.

"Not much talent?" asked her husband.

"In a way, they have talent, I suppose," she replied. "They sing like the Mormon Tabernacle rugby team."

The symphony musicians had little confidence in the person brought in to be their new conductor. Their fears were realized at the very first rehearsal. The conductor's wand was unsteady, and he had them playing at atrocious tempos and volumes. Soon, the sound became more dissonant than that of a first-year elementary school band.

The cymbalist had heard enough. During a delicate, soft passage, he suddenly clashed his instruments together with all the force and fury he could muster.

The music stopped. The conductor, highly agitated, looked angrily around the orchestra, demanding, "Who did that? Who *did* that?"

Jenny: "So you're a professional rock musician? That's exciting!"
Wally: "Yeah, I guess I've played the hits in half the nightclubs in New York City."
Jenny: "Why aren't you still playing music?"
Wally: "My quarters ran out."

An operatic tenor was consulting his doctor in desperation. "You've *got* to do something for this head cold," he demanded.

"I can give you medicine to relieve the symptoms," the doctor explained, "but you'll still have the cold. It simply has to run its course. You know that."

"But it won't do this week. Whenever I get a head cold, in a few days it goes to my throat, then to my chest—and I have my most important performance of the year coming up Friday night! I insist that you do something."

"Well, perhaps we can tie your neck in a knot until Friday. That might delay the cold's progress."

"I've swallowed my harmonica!" shrieked Jones.

"Good thing you don't play banjo," drawled the doctor.

What has eight hands and plays "Rocky Top"?
  A bluegrass band.

An inexperienced cello instructor began his first class nervously. He squawked a few melodies to demonstrate the sound of the instrument, then gave a brief lecture about the instrument.

"My own cello," he mentioned proudly, "is an exceptional instrument—quite expensive. Yours are only beginners' models, of course. But in the hands of a practiced musician, any cello will provide many years of rich, sonorous, exquisite music."

One student nudged another and said sadly, "I'm afraid some other practiced musician used up all the rich, sonorous, exquisite music his cello had, a long time ago."

NEIGHBORS

The best neighbors are the ones who make their loudest noises at the same time you're making yours.

"I think the Smiths are suffering from age-related strife," a woman said of her neighbors.

"What do you mean?" asked her husband.

"He won't act his age, and she won't admit hers."

The prospective buyer of a home in an exclusive subdivision had to appear before the neighborhood association's screening committee.

"Do you have small children?" was the first question.

"No."

"Outdoor pets?"

"No."

"Do you play any musical instrument at home?"

"No."

"Do you often host personal or business guests who might arrive in more than two vehicles at one time?"

"No." And by now, the prospect had decided the restrictions weren't for him. He held up his hand, rose from his chair, and told the panel, "We may as well call off the deal right now. You need to be aware I sneeze on the average of two or three times a week."

A secret agent was directed to a posh condominium complex to contact an anonymous source. "Williams is the name," he was told by his superior. "Hand him this envelope."

Arriving at the complex, he was confused to find four different Williamses occupying adjacent quarters. He decided to try the second condo. When a gentleman answered his knock, the agent spoke the pass code: "The grape arbor is down."

Looking him over, the man shook his head. "I'm Williams the accountant. You might try Williams the spy. Two doors down."

A door-to-door salesman approached a nice home where two children played in the front yard. "Are either of your parents home?" he called.

"Yeah, they're both home."

The salesman rang the bell and waited. He rang again. Still, no one answered the door.

"Why won't they come to the door?" he asked the children.

"This isn't our house," said one.

Policeman to Bystander: "I thought you said you saw a man jump from the top of the apartment complex."

Bystander: "Yes. It was poor old Larry. I recognized him from a distance."

Policeman: "We've searched the premises, and we couldn't find anyone."

Bystander: "Did you check inside? Knowing Larry, he probably had to stop and ask directions."

"I see the Andersons have returned our grill," said the wife happily, glancing out the window. "They've had it for the last six months, and I was afraid now that they're moving, they'd take it with them by mistake."

"You mean that was *our* grill?" screamed her husband, entering the back door. "I just paid them $25 for it at their yard sale!"

"Dad, I think the Browns next door are angry at us."

"Why is that?"

"They're probably mad because our dog can retrieve the newspaper, and theirs can't."

"How could you possibly know that? We don't even subscribe to the paper."

"Yeah, that's probably got something to do with it, too."

NONSENSE

A psychiatrist looked up to see, standing in the office doorway, a short, stout man stuffing a peanut butter sandwich into the beak of a parrot atop his head.

"What can I do for you?" the psychiatrist asked.

"Make him lose the sandwich!" hollered the parrot. "I hate peanut butter."

A baby hippopotamus was playing hide and seek in the jungle with an ant. The ant, logically, had an easier time concealing himself. Finally, in frustration, the young hippo deliberately stepped on the poor ant.

"Bruce!" shouted the hippo's mother, seeing what had happened. "Why did you kill that ant?"

"I only meant to trip him," Bruce said sheepishly.

A woman in Ireland happened to meet an old friend, who was blind, and asked how she was faring.

"Well," the blind woman said, "I've had to give up me skydivin'."

"Skydivin'! I didn't know ye could do that!"

"Oh, yes. And a fine time I was havin'. But it didn't agree with me dog."

A Martian spacecraft landed just outside a big American city. The crew managed to sneak into town without being noticed until one of the Martians saw a garbage truck round a corner too fast, throwing off a sheet of scrap metal. He automatically waved and yelled, "Hey, lady, you dropped your handkerchief!"

A man was playing chess with his dog on the backyard picnic table. A neighbor noticed. "Wow, I've never seen a dog play chess before. She must be very smart."

"Hah!" scoffed the dog's opponent. "Not so smart. I've beaten her four out of five games."

Ron: "Why do matadors wave bright red capes at bulls?"
Rachel: "To make the bulls angry so they'll charge."
Ron: "You mean bulls don't like bright red?"
Rachel: "Oh, bulls don't mind. It's chickens that don't like bright red."
Ron: "So what does that have to do with bullfights?"
Rachel: "A bull really hates being treated like a chicken."

A bear went into a shoe store. The clerk was amazed, watching the bear try on oversized loafers and wingtips. The bear found a pair of $50 loafers and gave the clerk a one-hundred-dollar bill.

Figuring the bear didn't understand money and math, the clerk handed back a ten-dollar bill and remarked, "You're the first bear I've ever had for a customer."

"And with your prices, I'm sure I'll be the last."

A horse nosed his way into a convenience store and asked for a pack of cigarettes.

"Are you eighteen?" asked the clerk.

Fred: "Wanna hear a couple of great jokes?"
Ted: "Sure."
Fred: "Great joke. Great joke."

Pam: "Did you know 'fat' and 'slim' are really the same thing?"
Sam: "Get outa here. They're the opposite."
Pam: "Then what's the difference between 'fat chance' and 'slim chance'?"

THE OUT-OF-DOORS

The story is told of Daniel Webster who, after a day of hunting, found himself far from home at nightfall. After groping through the darkness awhile, he came upon a farmhouse and knocked repeatedly at the door. It was several minutes before the farmer opened an upstairs window and held a lantern out to see who was down there.

"What do you want?" the farmer asked gruffly.

"I wish to spend the night here," Webster implored.

"Good. Spend the night there." The lantern went out and the window closed.

Michelle: "Mom! Mom! We just found a snake in the backyard!"
Mom: "Oh, no! Has it bitten anyone?"
Michelle: "Nah. Actually, it's just a baby. It's kinda cute!"
Mom: "Well, you know some snakes never grow very long. How can you be sure it's a baby?"
Michelle: " 'Cause it carries its own rattle at the tip of its tail."

Two retired friends were lounging at poolside when one commented, "I feel like hiking three miles in the mountains this weekend."

"Well, just stay in bed," the friend said. "The feeling will pass."

115

Mark: "The scoutmaster says he won't take me along on anymore camping trips."

Sharon: "Why not? What did you do?"

Mark: "I think he's angry because I lost the compass when we waded across the creek."

Sharon: "He's that mad just because a little compass got lost?"

Mark: "Well, it wasn't just the compass that got lost. We all got lost."

A hiker followed a trail out of the woods and found himself at a crossroads store. Disoriented, he approached a woman who stood outside.

"Can you tell me how far Hooterville is?" he asked.

"I'm afraid not."

"Well, which of these roads goes north?"

"I'm not sure."

The hiker was exasperated. "Don't you know anything? What village is this?"

"I don't know that, either. I'm just passing through."

An obscure, lofty peak in Alaska had never been scaled until two American climbers made it to the top after a grueling three-day ordeal. At the end their strength, they lay in the thin air and rested for several hours. Then, ready to begin the descent, one said, "Okay, let's plant the American flag and head back down."

The partner turned with a frown. "I thought you brought the flag."

PATIENCE

If evolution holds true, why hasn't nature produced a housewife who can vacuum the floor, answer the phone, help with the homework, and change the baby all at the same time? And why hasn't it produced a pedestrian who can dodge three vehicles at once?

A barber commented snidely as he cut a customer's hair, "A few grey hairs, I see."

"I don't doubt it," the gentleman said. "Please work a little faster."

PERSPECTIVE

"Dad, is it true people judge you by the company you keep?"

"I'm afraid so, Son."

"Well, then, if two guys hang out together, and one's good and the other's bad, does that mean people think the good guy is bad and the bad guy is good?"

"Your boyfriend is cute. I love that blond hair and those blue eyes."

"Yeah, he's got a twin, too."

"Really! Can you tell them apart easily?"

"Well, if you look close, you'll notice his sister's a brunette and a little shorter than him."

A couple and their small child made their way onto a crowded bus. There were no seats vacant, so they all had to stand in the aisle as the bus bounced along the streets.

The child was licking an ice cream cone, trying unsuccessfully to stay ahead of the melting vanilla mess. Unfortunately, the woman seated nearest the youngster wore an expensive fur coat. More than once, the ice cream brushed against the brownish-black fur.

When the woman finally noticed what was happening, she shrieked, "My coat! It has dreadful, sticky ice cream in it!"

Examining the ice cream cone, the child shrieked, "My ice cream! It's got hair in it!"

A dusty cowboy rode into town, shuffled into the barbershop, sank into the barber's chair, and said, "Gimme a shave, Partner."

"That'll be a mite hard, with your head slumped so low," the barber observed.

The cowboy pondered a minute. "All right," he said. "Then gimme a haircut."

Marcie has a master's degree in physical science. Each day, she asks, "Why does this work?"

Kevin has a master's degree in mechanical engineering. Each day, he asks, "How does this work?"

Brit has a master's degree in economics. Each day, she asks, "How much does it cost to manufacture this?"

Chuck has a master's degree in chemistry. Each day, he asks, "Could this be hazardous to the environment?"

Alvin has a master's degree in liberal arts. Each day, he asks, "Would you like that cheeseburger with everything?"

PETS

Two days after they'd moved into the neighborhood, the new family received a visit from a neighbor around the corner. "I'm very concerned," the neighbor said solemnly. "Your dogs are up barking all night long."

"Oh, they'll be quite all right," said the woman of the house. "They get plenty of sleep during the day."

"I've lost my place in the Jones household," lamented one cat to a neighbor cat.

"What happened?"

"The old man bought a laptop computer."

The phone rang at 2:00 in the morning. Groggily, the man of the house lifted the receiver and heard, "This is 330 Woodvine, next block over. You're dog's been howling for the last thirty minutes, and we can't get to sleep. Shut that animal up!"

Without waiting for a response, the caller hung up the phone.

The next night at 2:00 A.M., the aroused neighbor dialed up 330 Woodvine. When the owner answered, he pleasantly informed him, "We don't own a dog," and hung up.

A notice in a weekly newspaper advertised bulldog puppies. "Cute, already housebroken," the advertiser promised. "Eat most any food you put in front of them. Love children."

Mother caught little Davie feeding the dog under the table at suppertime again. "Davie," she fussed, "you know very well you're not supposed to feed the dog from our table food!"

"Yes, Ma'am," Davie confessed, hanging his head.

"Don't you understand why we have that rule in our house?"

Davie thought a moment. "I guess it's because if the dog doesn't like the food I hand it, the stuff will end up on the floor and eventually rot."

POTPOURRI

A man was lugging a grandfather clock from an antique shop to his car, three blocks away. Swaggering with each step, unable to see directly in front of him, he accidentally bumped an elderly couple heading in his direction on the sidewalk.

"I'm so sorry," he apologized, turning awkwardly toward them.

The couple glared at him angrily. The lady retorted, "Why don't you carry a wristwatch, like everyone else?"

Coming in from a drenching rain, a gentleman hung his coat on a crowded rack in the waiting room of a doctor's office. He called at the desk and was admitted shortly afterward for his scheduled appointment.

An hour and a half later, he emerged from his checkup and went to the rack for his coat. Plundering through the collection of wraps, he became annoyed, then angry. He was slinging coats on the floor furiously when the receptionist came to his assistance.

"I believe this one's yours, Mr. Tettleby," she said politely, holding up his coat. "See? It has your initials on the liner."

"Certainly not," refuted Mr. Tettleby. "My coat's soaking wet."

What do you call the wife of a duke?
A ducky.

"I see old Sen. Jones isn't quite as big a windbag as he used to be," said Elliott after a political rally.

"You think he's mellower these days?"

"Oh, no, but he's lost a little weight."

A Greek tailor in Chicago had a lighthearted routine for customers who brought in torn dress coats or pants for repair.

"Euripides?" he would ask. To which knowing regulars would respond, "That's right. Eumenides?"

Two English tourists in France walked past a towering statue of Napoleon. As they did, a squirrel hiding under one of the statue's ears tossed a nutshell fragment at the humans below. It landed lightly against the ear of one of them.

He brushed his ear and glared up at the statue, but failed to see the squirrel, or anything else that could have bombed him from above. "I do believe that statue spat at me," he told his companion.

"Well, I must say," intoned the other dryly, "it does seem to be a spitting image of the old boy."

A couple at a sprawling, three-state dog show were about to leave when they realized they hadn't yet seen any Labrador Retrievers. The man asked an attendant, "Can you tell us where to find the Labs?"

The attendant scratched his head. "Oh," he said blankly. "Next building. Men's on the right, ladies' on the left."

"I hear Sam Culpepper passed away last week."

"Yeah, he was right well off, too. I'd like to know how much property he left."

" 'Bout all of it, I expect."

A salesman approached the gate of a farmyard and was about to enter when he noticed a large dog under a shade bush, eyeing him. The salesman called out to see if anyone was home.

The farmer and his wife came to the front door. "Come on in," said the farmer with a friendly gesture.

"What about the dog?" asked the salesman, hesitating. "Will he bite?"

"Don't know. We just got 'im yesterday, and we're right eager to find out."

A couple were gathering items for a garage sale before relocating to a new home.

"Bah, here's a totally worthless item," said the husband bringing a fire extinguisher out of the closet.

"Why do you say it's worthless?"

"Well, we bought it at least five years ago, and we've never used it at all."

"Did you hear they buried Spatzkof, the world chess champion, yesterday?"

"No! I had no idea he was even dead."

"He wasn't dead, actually. But he was concentrating so hard, they thought he was."

"This," said the pharmacist, "is guaranteed to make hair start growing back within a week."

He handed a jar of cream over to a balding customer for examination.

"Works in less than a week, you say?" the man asked.

"As advertised," the pharmacist assured him.

The customer opened the jar, touched a bit of the cream to his finger, reached across the counter and rubbed it on the pharmacist's own bald spot. "I'll be back in a week," he said, "to see if you're telling the truth."

An American president once called a break from a long cabinet meeting and strolled onto the White House lawn to gather his thoughts. He placed a hand on a garden rail and stood staring across the grass. For five full minutes, the president didn't move a muscle.

"He's really torn by this one," one cabinet official said quietly to another. "I've never before seen him this deep in thought."

Another five minutes passed, and the nation's highest officials looked on nervously as the president continued to stand perfectly still.

Eventually, the chief executive motioned for his cabinet to gather around him at the rail. "See that squirrel out there?" he asked, pointing. "It hasn't flinched for more than ten minutes. I do believe it's dead."

Mary: "I hear Skip was a real hero when the office building caught fire. They say he led the whole staff safely outside."
Irvin: "Something like that. Actually, what I heard was that Skip was the first one out the door."

In a crowded cafeteria, a couple of businessmen saw two elderly women with their trays, wandering around and searching futilely for a vacant table.

"Come sit here," one of them told the nearest woman. "We're just finishing. You can have this table."

"Why, that's so very kind of you," the woman said, smiling. "I believe you're about the nicest young man I've ever met."

The other woman, making her way to join the first, pulled the young businessman aside. "Don't believe a word she tells you. I'm her guardian. I'm returning her to the mental institution this afternoon."

A woman paid $50 to a palm reader. "I'm in a crisis," she explained hurriedly. "Can you predict the next four or five months?"

"Certainly," replied the shyster, pocketing the money. "March, April, May, June, and July. For another twenty bucks, I'll take you to the end of the year."

"How'd you enjoy the county fair?" Grandma asked.

"Waste of time," reported Jennifer. "It was so small, it only had one bumper car."

"Dad, I want to be a salesman like you when I grow up."

"Oh, no. Sales are tough these days. You'll have a much better future in technology."

"But I think I'll have a great future in sales."

"Nope. The future's not what it used to be."

A man took a parcel notice to the post office counter and called for his package. The clerk was gone for several minutes, searching the rear of the post office for the package. At last, the clerk returned, scrutinizing the label of a large, fat, battered manila envelope.

"I think this one may be yours," the clerk said, "but the name seems to be obliterated."

"Not mine, then," said the customer. "My name is Welles."

A naval drill instructor was talking to new enlistees. "Now this is a dangerous maneuver, so you'd better listen slowly to what I'm about to tell you."

Whispered one recruit to another, "And what happens if we listen fast?"

PROBLEM SOLVING

An elderly gentleman was a hopeless insomniac, and his wife and grown children at length resorted to taking him to a hypnotist. The hypnotist had a remarkable record for being able to cure such ailments—but his services were not cheap. "We'll pay whatever it costs," the mother declared. "Not only is he unable to rest himself, but he's depriving me of my rest, too."

The hypnotist proceeded as expected. He had the patient recline comfortably and then sat before him, slowly waving a gold pocket watch from a chain. He waited a few minutes before speaking at all, simply moving the watch in slow, precise arcs.

"You are becoming very, very drowsy," he began. "Your body is tired. . . . Your mind is tired. . . . Your muscles are weary. . . . You need rest. . . . Complete rest. . ."

This stage—convincing the patient of his need for rest—lasted awhile before the hypnotist got to the root of the instructions. "And now you must rest. You must sleep. Your family will take you home and put you into your warm, comfortable bed. You will sleep without waking for exactly eight hours. This you must do every night for a month, at the end of which time you will come back to see me and we will talk again about rest. . . rest. . .beautiful, peaceful rest."

Softer and softer the hypnotist's voice became. Finally, each member of the family sitting around the room was almost asleep. The victim himself had closed his eyes and was beginning to snore.

"You may take him home now," the hypnotist quietly advised,

rousing the family. Ecstatic, they wrote a check for even more than the predetermined amount, and the hypnotist left the room.

The sons gently began to lift their father from the chair. Then he opened his eyes, glanced furtively around the room, and asked, "Is that imbecile finally gone?"

An aging mountain woman, pontificating on the foibles of international politics during World War II, was overheard to remark, "I wish Hitler would settle down and get married."

The little town had just acquired a state-of-the-art fire engine, and a debate warmed the next town council meeting over what to do with the venerable antique the new truck replaced. Some wanted to sell fragments as souvenirs. Some wanted to display it in a museum. Some said it should be scrapped.

At length, grizzled volunteer Charlie stood and silenced the contenders. "I move we keep the old truck in service," he proposed. "Use it for false alarms."

A little boy from the city was visiting his cousins on the farm. Milking cows particularly fascinated him. "I think I see how you get it going," he told his uncle after watching intently. "But how do you turn it off?"

PSYCHiATRY

Doctor: "Our testing shows you're clearly schizophrenic. You have twin personalities."
Patient: "Yes, one of me sees that clearly. But the other me wants a second opinion."

Bridgit: "You look worried."
Brodie: "I am. I'm convinced I'm losing my mind."
Bridgit: "Nonsense! What makes you think so?"
Brodie: "Well, I heard that one person in five suffers from a mental disorder. My four sisters are all normal, so it must be me."

The young, bearded man sat in the psychiatrist's office clapping his hands in a steady but strange cadence: *clap. . .clap-clap. . .clap. . . clap-clap. . . .*

When it came the young man's turn, the psychiatrist immediately asked him the meaning of the hand-clap routine.

"It's a secret ritual," the patient answered. "I learned it from a street musician."

"What's its purpose?"

"It keeps killer sharks away."

"Oh, you won't be bothered by a shark in here," assured the psychiatrist.

"Thanks to me," added the patient.

A psychiatrist prescribed a $90 bottle of pills and promised it would boost her patient's discernment and intelligence. A month later, the patient returned.

"Dr. Strathburn, I believe that medicine you prescribed is worthless. And I was very disturbed to learn you own stock in the drug company."

"See? You're wiser already."

"Doc, I've been having horrible dreams at night."

"What are they about?"

"Well, last night I dreamed I was in a pasture eating grass with a herd of cows."

"That's odd, but not really problematic. Why does it bother you?"

"When I got up this morning, the corner of my bed was missing."

What phone number do schizophrenics dial in an emergency?
911, 211, and 611.

"I'm so unhappy with myself," intoned a patient to her psychiatrist. "See those tomatoes growing in my hair?"

The psychiatrist decided to play along with the delusion for a moment. "Yes, I see. What's wrong with them?"

"Why, they represent yet another failure in my life."

"How do you mean?"

"I planted watermelons."

"Doctor, I just can't pull myself together."

"Sure you can. Now, sit right down and tell me precisely what your problem is."

"Well, you see, I'm a pair of curtains. . . ."

"So what seems to be your problem?"

"I think I'm going batty. I keep thinking this is Monday."

"Yes, this is Monday. You're cured. That'll be $50."

REAL ESTATE

A realtor was showing a lovely piece of retirement property to a sullen, bargain-minded couple. "Isn't that a spectacular view?" the realtor suggested, pointing across a sunlit valley of green.

"Hmph," said the man. "Apart from the mountains, what's there to see?"

A rancher was gazing across the vast expanse of the Grand Canyon for the first time in his life. "That," he remarked, "would be a mighty tough place to recover stray cattle."

RESTAURANTS

A diner shrieked when she saw a winged insect floating in her bowl of soup. "What's this?" she yelled at the waitress.

The waitress peered into the bowl. "I'd say it's either a small mosquito or a large gnat."

Joye: "Why don't we try the King's Palace for dinner? I've heard they have fabulous seafood entrées."
Walt: "Nah, too crowded. You have to wait two hours for a table. Nobody but nobody goes there nowadays."

Diner: "Waiter, this coffee tastes dreadful. Please bring me some hot tea, instead."
Waiter: "But that is hot tea."
Diner: "Then bring me some coffee."

Diner: "Would you please bring me some water?"
Waitress: "You mean drinking water?"
Diner: "No, actually, I thought I might take a bath."

SCHOOL

Mother: "How are you doing in math?"
Child: "I can handle some of the digits."
Mother: "What do you mean?"
Child: "The whole numbers are a bit of a bother, but I can figure the zeros correctly every time!"

Mother and father were writing out payments for the monthly bills one evening.

"Electricity, credit card interest, groceries—everything is going up!" exclaimed the father.

"Nothing ever goes down," agreed the mom.

"Take a look at this!" chirped their child, entering the room with her report card.

The fifth-grader was having so much trouble with his math homework that he finally had to call in his father for assistance. The next morning, he confidently turned the assignment in to his teacher.

Imagine his amazement when the paper was returned at the end of the day with a grade of 60/F.

"Hey!" the boy cried, rising from his desk. "You've flunked my dad!"

"What are algebraic symbols for?" a sixth-grader asked her high school sister.

"That's how the math teacher talks when he can't express himself in plain English."

Teacher: "What do you get when you multiply 63 times 14?"
Albert: "The wrong answer, I'm sure."

Donny came home from school one afternoon and, as required, handed his mother a discipline ticket the teacher had given him.

"Now, Donny, what did you do to get a discipline ticket?"

"I really dunno, Mom. Marv and Ellie were talking to me in science class, and the next thing I knew, I got caught."

Biology Teacher: "As you can see from these diagrams, there are thousands of miles of arteries, vessels, and blood veins in the human body."
Student: "I guess that's why old people have 'tired blood.' "

The teacher was giving her class a spelling quiz on animal words. With "aardvark," she thought it only fair to warn the students about the double "aa" at the beginning.

Unfortunately, the next word she called out was "anteater." When she graded the tests later, she found most of her students had spelled it "aanteater."

The father of a high school senior phoned the Latin teacher and demanded to know why his son had been given a grade of F on the midyear exam.

"Because we're not allowed to give a G," said the teacher.

A father looked on as his wife signed their son's report card. "Why are you signing each page with an 'X'?" he asked.

"You don't want his teachers to think anybody who's literate has a sixth-grader like that, do you?"

Teacher: "What is 24 times 8?"
Pupil: "192."
Teacher: "That's very good."
Pupil: "Whaddya mean, very good? It's absolutely perfect."

"Mark, can you give us an example of a double negative?" the English teacher asked.

Mark rubbed his chin and slowly shook his head. "I can't think of no double negatives."

A father was reviewing his daughter's report card with disapproval. "You don't seem to be working very hard," he commented.

"I work as hard as anybody else in class," she snapped.

"Well, your teacher doesn't seem very impressed."

"How do you expect us to impress somebody who's earned a master's degree?"

When Abraham Lincoln was a lad in school, he was known for being a good speller. One day a classmate was asked to spell the word "defied." She was intimidated by the stern schoolteacher and uncertain whether the word contained a "y" or "i" in the middle. But she noticed Lincoln smiling at her and pointing to his eye.

"D-e-f-i-e-d," she spelled correctly.

It's said she never forgot Lincoln's kindness—or the spelling of that word!

History Teacher: "Why was Washington standing in the bow of the boat as the army crossed the Delaware?"
Student: "Because he knew if he sat down, he'd have to row."

A student asked his geography teacher, "Can people in Ireland yell across the water to people in England?"

"Of course not. It's many miles between them."

"But it's less than an inch on this map."

On the first day of school, a freckle-faced lad handed his new teacher a note from his mother. The teacher unsealed the note, read it, looked at the child with a frown, and placed the note inside a desk drawer.

"So what did she write?" the boy asked.

"It's a disclaimer."

"A what?"

"It says, 'The opinions expressed by Leo are not necessarily those of his mother and father.'"

The regularly tardy high school student ran into geometry class a minute after the bell rang, slamming the door behind him. He noisily collapsed into his desk and slammed his book bag to the floor.

"Ken, what kind of behavior is that?" the teacher demanded. "You've distracted everybody. You know you should walk in school, not run."

"But you told me last week I'd be suspended if I walked into your class late one more time."

"The word 'corpse' has an 'e' on the end," the teacher corrected a spelling student. "Don't you know the difference between a 'corps' and a 'corpse'?"

"I think so," the student answered. "I believe a corps is a dead man, and a corpse is a dead woman."

A first-grade teacher had instructed her students to draw examples of rings. She slowly walked around the room, examining their ideas. At Will's desk, she stopped in surprise.

"But Will," she said, "those are all squares and rectangles."

"No, they're not," Will protested. "They're boxing rings."

A fifth-grader was ordered to the back of the line for rowdiness while waiting to enter the school lunchroom. A minute later, he resumed his old place.

"What are you trying to do?" asked the teacher monitoring the lunch line. "I sent you to the rear."

"I went, but there's already somebody back there."

A teacher caught a student chewing gum in class.

"Who gave you the gum?" the teacher asked.

"I don't remember."

"How long have you been chewing it?"

"Not very long."

"Haven't you been caught doing that before?"

"Now and then, I suppose."

"Okay, go stand in the corner."

The student was concerned, because the recess bell was about to ring. "How long do I have to stay here?"

The teacher smiled. "Just for awhile."

"Jim, where's your lunch box?" the teacher asked.

"Oh, I ain't got none. I'm eating in the cafeteria."

"No, no, Jim. You say, 'I don't have a lunch box. You don't have a lunch box. Sally doesn't have one. We don't have any.' "

Jim looked puzzled. "So, what happened to all the lunch boxes?"

"How was your first day of school?" Mother asked Wanda. "Tell me all about it!"

"It was a complete waste of time. I'm dropping out."

"Oh, no! What went wrong?"

"I just don't see any point to it. I still can't read. Can't write. And I'm not allowed to say anything to anybody."

SCIENCE

"I have just developed the most powerful acid compound known to humans," a scientist announced to her colleagues. "There is only one problem."

"What is that?" asked one.

"Finding a container for it."

A traveler in Montana stopped at an isolated, weather-beaten store. Behind the cash register was a large, colorful chunk of petrified wood.

"I'd love to know how old a piece of wood like that is," remarked the traveler.

"It's exactly two million and fourteen years old," said the grizzled proprietor.

"How can you be so precise?"

"A geology professor stopped in here and told me it was a two-million-year-old rock. That was fourteen years ago."

"Every inanimate object on the face of the earth falls into either of two categories," an engineering professor proposed in a lecture. "One, they are objects that immediately require fixing, or two, they are objects that require fixing after humans have tinkered with them."

SECRETARIES

A legal secretary returned to work after a two-week vacation and sarcastically asked a colleague, "So how'd that hotshot temp work out while I was gone?"

"Pretty bad. He couldn't type more than thirty-five words a minute. Kept pestering us with the simplest questions about using the word processor. Didn't know how to alternate the paper bins in the printer. Made the coffee too strong. Embarrassed the managing partner in front of some of our clients. Oh—and he was one of the worst gossips we've ever had."

"Just as I figured," sneered the veteran triumphantly.

"Yes, it was pretty much as though you hadn't left."

"I'm going to play golf," the boss said, "but you can just tell callers I'm in a meeting."

To which the secretary replied, "I'll be your receptionist, but not your deceptionist."

The secretary entered a crowded elevator at the end of the day, headed for home. Without thinking, she pressed the ground floor button twice in rapid succession.

Another secretary noticed and commented knowingly, "You must keep your hand on a computer mouse all day, too."

A boss ended the day with instructions to the secretary for tomorrow.

"I've just finished dictating about forty letters; type them up and get them in the mail. You also need to go to the office supply store and take notes on those three new fax/printer models so we can choose one and get the purchase approved right away. Barnes is coming in at 2:00, and she'll want you to go through the new shipping contracts with her—but get her out of here by 3:30 so you can take notes at the staff meeting. Oh, Wilkins wants you to have the contact database updated and distributed before the meeting—and please type up my committee report; I'll try to have it dictated by late morning. Martin's computer is on the blink; he needs you to look at it, first thing. And don't forget to show Abercrombie how to key in the title insurance information on the new forms.

"Think you can manage all that?"

"Sure," said the secretary, not batting an eye. "I'll bring my TV set, in case I get bored."

SOLDIERS

A rural mail carrier at the end of World War II took the news of the armistice to an isolated mountain family. He thought the good tidings would bring smiles, but the woman on the porch shook her head sadly.

"I s'pose it figures," she grumbled.

"What do you mean?" asked the carrier.

"We sent our Jeb off to join the army two months ago."

"Looks like he missed all the fightin'."

"That's what I mean. That boy never could hold a job."

A general was inspecting a line of recruits. "Where ya from, Son?" he asked one lad.

"Pennsylvania, Sir!" barked the nervous soldier.

"Which part?"

"Uh—all of me, Sir!"

A class of paratrooper recruits took to the air on their first free-fall jump. At the designated altitude, they opened their chutes—but one late jumper streaked past them, the handle of the ripcord loose in his hand.

"Hey, are you okay?" shouted a shocked comrade.

"So far," came the reply.

Recruiting Officer: "What do you mean you want to join the Marines? You're still in high school. You're practically an infant!"

Teenager: "Yes, Sir. I'd like to join the infantry."

In the late 1940s, a veteran of World War II applied for a bank job. During the interview, the unsmiling, no-nonsense bank official fired question after question, taking notes and never glancing up at the veteran.

"Most recent job position?" was the question.

"Supply officer," the applicant replied.

"Duration of employment?"

"Three and a half years."

"Reason for termination?"

The applicant thought about it a moment and then answered, "We won the war."

An army unit on training maneuvers hacked through heavy underbrush to the edge of a river. "Have you found a shallow place for us to cross over?" the lieutenant asked the platoon scout.

"Yes, Sir, about a hundred yards downstream."

The soldiers were exhausted when they made their way to the crossing point. Wading into the stream, they soon dropped into a deep hole. The whole platoon floundered in the current and gasped for breath.

"I thought you said this place was shallow!" the officer sputtered.

"Well, Sir, I watched the ducks go all the way across, and it only came up to the tops of their legs."

The story is told of a Civil War unit on patrol who'd lived on miserable hardtack for days. The soldiers were naturally excited when they spied a chicken on the road ahead of them. One of the privates broke and ran after the chicken.

"Halt!" shouted his lieutenant.

The soldier kept running.

"Halt, I say!" the officer repeated, angered by this display of insubordination.

The private pressed his pursuit of the chicken.

"Halt or I'll shoot!" the lieutenant cried, drawing his pistol.

Just at that moment, the soldier caught the chicken, snapped its neck, and began toting it back toward his comrades. "I'll teach you to halt when the lieutenant orders you to halt!" he chided his newfound meal.

Morgan: "My great-great-great-grandfather fought with General Custer."

Mitchum: "I don't doubt it. Your family'll fight anybody."

An army troop had been on patrol more than a week. The soldiers were smelly and filthy.

One morning an order came down the ranks for them to change socks. "But we don't have any clean socks," said one of the men.

"Colonel's orders," said the sergeant. "He insists on cleanliness in the field. We all have to change socks."

The soldiers looked at each other, bewildered. After a minute, one of them had an idea. "Okay, Jefferson, you change with me. Bilinsky, you change with Carmichael. . . ."

What did the frightened soldier do when a land mine tore up the main road?

He tore up a side path.

"We received our uniforms today," a recruit wrote to his mother from boot camp. "It made me feel very proud, although the pants are a little too loose around the chest."

SPORTS

A golfing duffer cringed when his drive landed in an anthill. Choosing a sand wedge, he positioned himself and slashed at the half-buried ball. Sand and ants flew. The ball wasn't touched.

Again the novice braced and swung. Again the ant hill was devastated, but the ball lay unmoved.

Among the panic-stricken ant colony, one ant yelled to a buddy, "Follow me! That big white ball there seems to be a pretty safe place!"

Returning home from a round of golf, a man was asked by his cheery wife, "Did you win today, Honey?"

"Of course not," he muttered. "You know I was playing against the boss."

Roger was just beginning to get over the unique tragedy of losing his golfing buddy, who'd dropped dead of a heart attack on the fairway some weeks earlier.

"It must have been terribly hard carrying him back to the clubhouse like you did," remarked a friend. "I understand he was a big man."

"Weighed about 230," Roger acknowledged. "And it was ninety degrees that day. Yeah, it was rough. Pick him up, find the ball, put him down, take my next shot. Pick him up, find the ball. . . ."

A college crew team had spent the whole afternoon rowing and were near exhaustion. Heading for the locker room, they were stopped by the team captain.

"Fellows, I have some good news and some bad news," he said. "The good news is you're to take a twenty-minute break, and then the college president is coming down here to watch you perform."

The rowers groaned. "So what's the bad news?" one asked sarcastically.

"He's bringing his water skis."

"I like the statistics of your quarterback, Evans," a pro scout told a college football coach. "What's your opinion of him personally?"

"Good skills. Sort of a *prima donna*, though."

"How do you mean?"

"Well, let's just say when he makes a big play, he's a big advocate of the idea of taking personal responsibility for the way things happen. When he gets sacked, he's a big advocate of the concept of luck."

Marge: "What inspired you to take up skydiving?"
Sue: "I was a passenger in a plane that ran out of gas at five thousand feet."

TALL TALES

Graham: "I hear your town weathered a terrible flood last week."
Bell: "Yeah, the mousetraps in our basement caught three fish."

William was notorious for stretching the truth outrageously. When he caught a fish, it quickly grew to three, five, eight, ten pounds, as he repeated the story. A slight accident became a near-death experience, in his words.

One day his minister sat down with him and warned sternly of the dangers—both in this life and eternally—of constant lying. "When you feel the urge to embellish the facts," the clergyman suggested, tapping the cover of his Bible, "remember the Good Book."

The next day, William was telling friends about a stranger he'd just seen come out of the police station. "He had to have been six feet ten inches. Fists the size of basketballs. Biceps like stovepipes. Mean-looking. I saw a glimmer of metal in the back of his car, and I'm sure it was a submachine gun."

William's minister had been standing nearby, unnoticed. He stepped forward and asked loudly, "And how much do you reckon this fellow weighed?"

William, dumbfounded, spotted the preacher's black Bible. "Er, I guess about ninety pounds."

TEENAGERS

Kelley, sobbing: "I'm just devastated. No one has replied to my party invitations—and it's tonight!"
Dottie: "Well, if nobody wants to come, you can't stop them."

When your teenage children have friends in distant cities, you become much more concerned about obscene phone bills than you are about obscene phone calls.

"When Abraham Lincoln was your age," a man said to his lazy teenage son, "he was chopping wood, plowing, and hunting for food."

"When he was your age," the boy responded, "he was president of the United States."

"What's the most difficult age to get a child to sleep regularly?" a new mother asked an older veteran of child rearing.

"About seventeen years."

TRAVEL

A guest at a second-class motel repeatedly rang the desk clerk late at night, each time to be placed on hold while the clerk juggled other calls. The guest would lose his patience with the permahold routine, hang up, and redial a few minutes later.

Finally, the clerk actually took his call—and didn't hesitate to express annoyance at the repeated rings. "This is about the fifth time you've rung me," the clerk began sternly. "You seem to have an incurable itch. What in the world is eating you?"

"Something in this carpet is, for sure," the guest agreed. "I think I have a right to know what it is."

"I just returned from Germany and had the most wonderful time," bubbled Ginger to her friends.

"I thought before you left, you said you were having trouble with your German," Melody said.

"Oh, I spoke fluently. It was the Germans who had trouble with it."

"What kinds of papers do I need to travel to Europe?" a youth asked a travel agent.

"Basically, a passport and a visa."

"I have the passport, no problem. Do you think they'll accept Mastercard?"

A stout businessman took his suitcase from the luggage ramp at the Fresno airport and huffed to the airline's courtesy desk.

"What's the meaning of this?" he demanded, showing the agent the large, red-lettered handling tag tied to his suitcase handle. "I'm well aware of my weight problem, but what right does your airline have to comment on it in public?"

The agent read the tag: FAT.

"That," she explained, "is the destination code for this airport."

A man in a tour group thought he had mastered French well enough to speak for himself. With his guide standing by, he approached a couple of Parisians and struck up an eloquent conversation. The locals, however, didn't respond to his questions. At length, the villagers began conversing with each other in low voices.

"I give up," the tourist admitted to the guide. "What are they saying?"

"They're debating whether you were speaking English or German."

A woman phoned a travel agent and demanded, "I need your finest accommodations in Ocala, Florida, for the week of the 20th."

After a moment, the agent suggested, "I can book you a penthouse suite in the heart of town. First class in every respect."

"With a beachfront view, I assume."

"Er, no ma'am. Ocala isn't near the ocean."

"Don't give me that!" the woman snapped. "I've seen it on a map. Florida is a narrow state."

The college student was quite nervous on the first afternoon of his summer job as a resort hotel porter. A veteran at the bell desk gave him some friendly advice: "You'll get good tips if you chat with the guests and call them by name."

"Er, how do I find out their names? Do I sneak over to the reception desk before I take them to their room, or just come right out and ask them?"

"No, no. Neither. All you have to do is notice the name and address labels on their suitcases."

With this advice, the student porter escorted a well-dressed, elderly couple to their suite on the fourth floor. Reaching down to clutch a couple of bags, he slyly read the tag dangling off one of the handles.

"So," he ventured, "it's nice having you here, Mr. and Mrs. Leather. What brings you to the islands?"

"How much will it cost me to fly to Dublin?" a man asked an airline ticket agent in Reno, Nevada.

After examining the database for different times and connections, the agent pointed out, "The lowest rates would involve long layovers in Denver and New York."

"Oh, it doesn't matter how long it takes. Just get me the lowest fare."

The agent punched a few more keys and came up with the reply: "Thirteen hundred and forty dollars, one way."

The man rubbed his chin. "That's still rather much, for me. What would it cost if I were to fly to New York and then connect with a train for the run over to Dublin?"

WEATHER

A man was driving home from an out-of-town trip and called his wife on the cellular phone. "I'll be home in about three hours," he observed. "I see the weather report calls for a 20 percent chance of snow flurries there tonight."

"Well, you'll need to drive more carefully than you think," his wife said. "The children have been building 20 percent snowmen and having 20 percent snowball fights since lunchtime."

News Anchor: "So what's the chance of rain today?"
Climatologist: "Oh, no worse than 50 percent."
Anchor: "And what's the chance you're wrong?"
Climatologist: "About the same."

After months of discouraging failures in his daily weather forecasts, a TV climatologist submitted his resignation.

"But you have such a friendly screen presence," the station manager protested. "Our audiences love you, even when you get the forecasts wrong."

"Thanks, but I really think I need to be in a different locale altogether."

"Why?"

"Well, it's obvious that the weather here just doesn't agree with me."

WIT & WISDOM

Skip: "Stupid people are always sure of themselves. Smart people question everything."
Rip: "Are you sure about that?"

When antique dealers get together, how do they strike up a conversation? Does one of them venture, "What's new?"

Has anyone noticed that it now costs more to entertain the average teenager than it cost to put both of the youth's parents through college?

Necessity is the mother of invention—even though much of what's invented is hardly necessary.

Grandpop: "Lincoln was right when he said, 'You can fool all the people some of the time and some of the people all the time.'"
Grandson: "But what happens the rest of the time?"
Grandpop: "They're likely to make fools of themselves, I reckon."

The primary difference between wives and husbands is that the former never forget special occasions and the latter never remember.

A good sermon is one that goes in one ear, out the other—and smacks somebody else right between the eyes.

A lot of government policies make about as much sense as interstate highways in Hawaii.

Abraham Lincoln remarked that common folks are the best in the country. "That is the reason the Lord made so many of them."

There's no such thing as a beautiful newborn baby—until you become a parent.

Why is it you can buy cigarettes at a gas station—where smoking is strictly forbidden?

To a kid with a hammer, everything in life is a nail.

It's always better to say nothing and have people wonder about your intelligence than to say something stupid and leave them no doubt.

"As your grandpa always said, if it ain't broke, don't fix it," the father told his son, a college engineering student.

"As my professor always says, if it ain't broke, it doesn't have enough features," parried the student.

How can time be such a wonderful healer—but such a terrible beautician?

If it goes without saying. . .then let it go.

Grandmom: "You should pay attention and try to learn from the mistakes of others."
Granddaughter: "Why?"
Grandmom: "Well, nobody's ever lived long enough to make all the mistakes in person."

Spinach is nothing more than cabbage with muscle; mustard greens are cabbage with a biblical tradition; and cauliflower greens are cabbage with a university degree.

THE WORKPLACE

"What do you mean I'm not qualified?" demanded a job applicant. "I have an IQ of 150. I scored 1,480 on the SAT. I graduated magna cum laude in graduate school."

"Yes," replied the hiring supervisor, "but we don't really require intelligence around here."

Boss: "This office looks as though it hasn't been cleaned for a month."
Maid: "That's not my fault. I only started work Monday."

Boss: "Why are you always late getting to work?"
Employee: "Well, it's been my experience that it helps make the day go by more quickly."

"Good news and bad news," reported an employee representative returning to the job after a weekly meeting with management.

"Give us the bad news first," mumbled a colleague.

"They're canceling the company's fire insurance policy."

"And the good news?"

"They're buying us a fire truck."

"What special skills do you have?" a company official asked a job applicant.

"Well, none, actually," admitted the applicant.

"I'm afraid we can't use you, then. We have several unskilled positions, but they're all filled right now by the president's relatives."

A dynamite explosion at a road construction site sent old Bill flying into oblivion. A few minutes later, the foreman came around to find out what had happened.

"Where's old Bill?" he asked.

"He left," said a coworker.

"When did he say he'd be back?"

"He didn't say. But if he comes back as quick as he left, I'd say he'll be back about five minutes ago."

Job Interviewer: "What were your three strongest subjects in college?"
Applicant: "Italian, German, and trigonometry."
Interviewer: "Let me hear you say 'good day' in Italian."
Applicant: "*Buon giorno.*"
Interviewer: "And in German? . . ."
Applicant: "*Guten Tag.*"
Interviewer: "And in trigonometry? . . ."

Boss: "Why are you sitting around loafing?"
Worker: "Sorry. I didn't realize you were here."